HIGH HOPES

Born in Swords, Dublin, in 1988, Steve Garrigan is the lead singer and songwriter of Irish rock band Kodaline. With fellow band mates Mark Prendergast, Jason Boland and Vinny May Jr, Steve has toured and performed in sold-out venues throughout the world, including the US, Asia, India and South Korea, as well as in Ireland and Europe. Kodaline's albums include *In a Perfect World* (2013), *Coming Up for Air* (2015), *Politics of Living* (2018) and *One Day at a Time* (2020). They have had numerous songs featured in TV shows and movies, and have close to two billion streams on Spotify alone. Steve lives in Dublin.

HIGH HOPES

Making Music, Losing My Way, Learning to Live

Steve Garrigan

HACHETTE
BOOKS
IRELAND

First published in Ireland in 2021 by
HACHETTE BOOKS IRELAND

3

Cataloguing in Publication Data is available from the British Library

ISBN 9781529347937

Typeset in Arno Pro by Bookends Publishing Services, Dublin

Printed and bound in Great Britain by Clays Ltd, Elcograf, S.p.A

Hachette Books Ireland policy is to use papers that are natural, renewable
and recyclable products and made from wood grown in sustainable forests.
The logging and manufacturing processes are expected to conform to
the environmental regulations of the country of origin.

Hachette Books Ireland
8 Castlecourt Centre
Castleknock
Dublin 15, Ireland

A division of Hachette UK Ltd
Carmelite House, 50 Victoria Embankment, EC4Y 0DZ

www.hachettebooksireland.ie

This book is dedicated to my dad, my mam, to my brother Al, and my two sisters, Fiona and Denise.

And to my friends.

And to my girlfriend, Diana, who has supported me through everything.

A special thanks to Neil Fetherstonhaugh
who helped shape the stories and memories in this book.

PROLOGUE

I DEBATED WITH MYSELF FOR A LONG TIME whether or not I should do this book because I felt I was too young to write about my life.

To be honest, this is something I never thought I'd have the courage to do. But I'm glad I did. Writing this book, for me, has been a therapeutic exercise and I hope that it also encourages anyone out there who might also be suffering to be brave, and seek help. You know, you only get one chance at life and there's no point in wasting it feeling miserable.

That's the mistake I made. I have lived with anxiety and depression pretty much all my life. It has affected everything I've ever done or achieved. And for a long time I suffered in silence. I just bottled everything up and didn't talk to anyone about it. I know now, of course, that that's what causes a lot of the harm. But I didn't know that then.

I'm still a bit insecure, a bit unsure of myself. That might seem strange, coming from somebody who makes their living getting up on stage and performing in front of tens of thousands of people, but that's just the way I was for a long time.

And the only time when I didn't feel like this was when I stood up and sang a song. Put a microphone in front of me and a guitar in my hands, and I could let go and feel real joy, if only for a few moments at a time. And because it was something that just came naturally to me, it meant I was able to get up in front of people and perform, without overthinking or worrying about it too much.

But when I wasn't singing or performing, I struggled to ignore all these other uncomfortable feelings that would bubble up. I just kept pushing them away, trying not to get caught up in them. It's something I've always struggled with, and still do. But when I was 20 years of age it would lead to my first serious panic attack.

It was a horrible experience. It turned my life upside down and for a while it completely stole my confidence. But it would also prove to be a turning point because it forced me to eventually reach out and get help.

Now, I sometimes stop and think, *If I had never had that panic attack, would I be where I am today?* Probably not. Because it was then, at my lowest point, that I decided to throw everything I had into songwriting. And for a long time it was the only thing I had in my life that kept me afloat.

1

July 1996

I'm around eight years of age and about to step up on stage for the first time in my life. It's the early afternoon and I'm sitting with my family in a pub in Courtown, a seaside town in County Wexford, where we had gone for the weekend.

My parents don't drink but they had brought us to the 'local', one of those places that every corner of Ireland has, where sometimes there would be a carvery and families would go to have something to eat on a Sunday afternoon.

They were a lot different back then though, with everyone sitting around smoking, for a start, and I'm sure the laws or whatever have changed now, but it was like a playground for the kids, who were allowed to run amok. There was also, usually, a little stage in the corner of the lounge area, where sometimes a guy would sit on a stool and play a few cover songs on a guitar or a keyboard while a drum machine kept the beat in the background.

There was a guitarist there that day, strumming his guitar and singing the Tom Jones song 'Delilah', badly, but they also had a karaoke machine set up and when the guitar guy took a break they were asking people to come and sing a song. Now, my family loves karaoke. My dad had brought a karaoke machine home one time, around Christmas, and we all used to take turns singing, so I had a bit of practice and I knew a couple of songs. My dad, who was always into having a bit of fun, was trying to get me to go up and sing one. I was like, 'Okay, I'm going to do this,' but I'll be honest, I was shitting it.

Nervously I went over to the man with the microphone and asked him to put on my favourite Bee Gees song. He asked me my name and said, 'Ladies and gentlemen, a big round of applause for Stephen, from Swords. And Stephen's going to sing 'Words' for us', and he selected the track and it came on.

The place was packed and I remember all these faces looking back at me but as soon as the music started all my nerves went away. The words came up on the screen but I didn't even have to look at them. I knew that song so well because it was my party piece that I would have sung at home loads of times before. But while I was a little performer in front of my family, this was the first time that a crowd of strangers was the audience. I closed my eyes and everything seemed to go quiet, like all the noise, all the voices and chatter died down. I remember trying not to choke on the smoke from all the cigarettes. And then that lovely piano intro started and I launched into the song at the top of my voice. I started moving and swaying as I got into the song and found myself lost in the moment as I belted out that big chorus.

There I was, this little eight-year-old kid, belting out one of the classics and I was just loving it. Before I knew it, the song was over and I was handing the mic back. I think there was even a brief round of applause but I'm not sure if anybody was really listening. The compère, I suppose you'd call him, came over clapping his hands and he handed me a little Casio watch. Now, this wasn't a competition or anything like that, I think he just thought, *Ah, I'd better give the little lad something for his efforts*, but I was delighted. I took my new prize back to my family, who were all laughing and cheering, and I remember being chuffed with myself. Not only for getting that watch but also because well, maybe it was then, after that little performance in Courtown that day, that something went off in my head: 'Okay, I can actually do this', you know? It occurred to me that I could really sing and people seemed to enjoy it. Well, maybe they did and maybe they didn't and they just gave me the watch because they felt sorry for me, but it was still a big deal for a shy kid like me.

Most kids are shy to some degree or another but I was incredibly introverted back then. I had always been uncomfortable around people I didn't know, and this discomfort made me nervous. I was very insecure, I suppose, as a kid and so I was very quiet and reserved. It's taken me years to fully accept that that's just who I am. I'm an introvert. But through therapy and self-acceptance I've come to terms with that and I'm happier for it.

I had felt like that for as long as I could remember so that was normal to me. But when I was put behind a microphone, I felt different. I was able to let all that go and relax, even for a few moments.

For most people, I'd imagine, getting up in front of a crowd, even a small one, would be a bit nerve-wracking, and it was for me too, but once I had that mic in my hand and I was singing a song I knew well, that nervousness, that anxiety which was always bubbling away under the surface would ease and I'd feel different. Better, somehow. I had experienced that feeling before, long before I got on that stage in Courtown, because I had already been singing at home with my family for years.

I grew up in River Valley in Swords, a town just outside Dublin, with my mam Maura, who was a teacher in the primary school I went to, my dad Des, who worked in a psychiatric hospital, my brother Alan who is four years older than me, and my two sisters, Denise who is one year older than me, and Fiona who is a year younger.

We were a close-knit family and we spent most of our time together growing up. I suppose, once we became teenagers, myself and my brother and my sisters were like anybody else, and we would kinda have our own friends and that, but as kids we got on well. Of course, there was always the odd time we would eat the heads off each other, either me and one of my sisters or my brother, over stupid things. But off the top of my head I can't think of any big arguments, it was always just who wanted to watch what on TV. Tiny things like that.

I had a happy enough childhood, I don't remember any big dramas, but I did run away from home once. I didn't know any of this had happened until I was told about it years later but apparently, when I was only two, I got out onto the road. Somehow I got down into the valley, which is a good, long distance away from our house, and a neighbour of ours, Sean

Joyce, found me. Now that I think about it, I do remember being delighted and wanting to keep going, to keep running. But he grabbed me and said, 'What the hell are you doing out here?' and he brought me back home. I don't know how I got out, maybe I let myself out or maybe the door was open, but I do know I made it as far as the valley. And I was probably lucky that nothing happened to me along the way. I was also always falling down the stairs and banging my head. Some of my friends say today that that explains a lot. I fell down four, maybe five times, my parents told me, and one of those times, they had to bring me to get stitches in my head. The second I got back home, I fell down the stairs again and I had to go back to the hospital for more stitches. My poor parents, for them it was blink and he's gone. I would be in my cot and I'd figure out how to escape. They had no idea how I was doing it but apparently I was taking the bars out and getting out that way.

There was always music in the house when I was growing up. All my family, in their own way, are into music or performing. Some of my earliest memories are of sitting in the back seat of my dad's car and listening to a compilation CD he had made himself. He had picked out all his favourite songs from all the albums he had in the house and burnt them onto this CD so that he could listen to them when he was driving.

Whenever we went anywhere in the car he'd stick on this CD and I'd be in the back seat, maybe five, six years of age, and I'd be singing along. To this day, I know every word to every song that was on that CD because I had learned them by singing them over and over. I'd grow to love all those old-school songs. There was Billy Joel, Bruce Springsteen, Jackson Browne and a song by Bob Dylan's son's band The Wallflowers called 'One Headlight'. There were some Neil Young songs too, and one was called 'Words (Between the Lines of Age)'. Now, that is a great song. I'm not sure what it is about that song in particular, but it hit me in a way I find hard to explain. Neil Young would write from a deep place about issues that affected him deeply and that song has an emotional depth to it that even as a kid I could pick up on. There was this raw emotion in his voice and I'd just get lost in it. And still, to this day, that's the sort of music I naturally gravitate towards. I wouldn't just sing the lyrics to all these songs either. I'd be sitting there, humming along to the melodies and imitating the instrumental parts. You know, it would come to the guitar solo and I'd be like, 'wah, wah, wah', and when it came to the drums I'd wave my arms in the air and go, 'dum, dum, bedum, dish'. God knows what my dad and the others in the car were doing while I was making all this racket, I'm just glad I didn't cause a crash.

From a very early age, then, I was learning about songs and exploring music. I think I was still only about eight or nine when I bought my first album, with my pocket money. It was Elvis Presley, a live album from 1957 or something like that, that I bought in Tape to Tape, a record shop that used to be in Swords, in the mall. It had all the classics on it. Like, there was his cover of 'Tutti Frutti' and 'Heartbreak Hotel'. I'm not sure why I chose Elvis, because my brother had already introduced me to The Beatles. And I was blown away by them. He had those records, ya know, the Blue Album and the Red Album? I remember hearing 'Revolution' for the first time and that big John Lennon scream at the start, and instantly all the hairs on the back of my neck stood up. Myself and my brother shared a bedroom and I nearly fell off the top bunk the first time I heard it. I jumped down and was like, 'What the heck is thaaaat?' It was the scream that got me. I'd never heard anything like that before and I just felt the amazing energy of that sound. My brother told me about them and who they were and we'd go through all the back catalogue: 'Back in the USSR', 'Ticket To Ride', 'She Loves You' …

I'm not sure, then, why I had gone for an Elvis album when I went to the record shop. There were other Elvis records in the house that I had listened to and maybe that's why I bought that one. All I knew was that if anything else sounded like

'Revolution', I wanted to hear it. Then my brother figured out Napster and how you could download music illegally.

Looking back now, as a musician and a songwriter, it's not something I'm particularly proud of, because I know how important royalties are to artists. Downloading music from sites like Napster is essentially stealing, but of course I know that now and didn't understand that then. But all of a sudden we had access to a whole world of music. One of the first songs I heard on Napster was Chuck Berry's 'Johnny B. Goode', that was also in the movie *Back to the Future*. I loved that movie and when I saw Michael J. Fox doing that big solo in the scene where he's on the stage in the hall, that just floored me. I was like, 'Woah, I wanna do that.' I wanted to get on a stage and do a solo like that. 'Johnny B. Goode' would be one of the first songs I'd learn to play properly on the guitar, and when we got our first band together it was the first song I'd ever play on stage. And I tried to play it just like Michael J. Fox did.

I had first learned how to perform at home, on my dad's karaoke machine, with my family. Christmas is amazing with my dad. He's the life and soul of the party and he likes taking the piss out of himself and entertaining people, in his own quirky way. He'll burst into song and then get everyone to join in, even at home. And he loves karaoke. He has his party pieces, those one or two songs that are like his 'go-to' songs, and to this day, if we're out anywhere together and there's a karaoke machine in the corner, we'll all be saying, 'Go on, Dad, get up and sing.' He's always like, 'No, no, no,' insisting he doesn't want to, and then you look around and he's knocking out Tom Jones and Frank Sinatra. And when he's finished and he gets his round of applause he's like, 'Will I do another?' It's a very funny thing to see.

And then, when he brought his own karaoke machine home that time at Christmas, when I was about six or seven, we'd all go into the sitting room and he'd encourage each of us to sing a song. We'd take it in turns to select one on the screen, press the button and start singing when the words appeared. One of my favourites was 'When the Going Gets Tough' by Billy Ocean and I'd sing it whenever we got together, which was most nights of the week. Those nights were great fun, but even if nobody else was around I'd still go into the sitting room on my own, put it on and sing away. I'd even sing it when we went over to my nan, Máiréad Duffy, who lives on the southside, in Glenageary. She's my mam's mam and she's an awesome lady. Originally from Kerry, she was a school teacher, like my mam. She is this larger-than-life character, who has her own creative streak. Her first language is Irish, and she writes poetry. She had all these poetry books lying around the house and three of her Irish poems were published in *Bí ag caint* in 1993 for the Junior Cert Irish exam, which I thought was pretty cool. We'd get in the car to go visit Nana Duffy at Christmas and on other family occasions. Me and my brother and sisters would run around the house with our cousins while my parents and aunts and uncles would gather in the sitting room. My nan is incredibly creative, very much about expressing yourself, be it through writing, painting, poetry or music, and she encouraged that creative streak in all of us. There would be fifteen or sixteen of us in her house, and then we'd all have to take turns to stand up and tell a story or read a poem to the whole family. My nan would start off by reading a poem and then maybe an uncle would tell a joke or two. Then a cousin might do a dance. Another uncle Mick had a guitar and my brother Alan had one that he'd got for Christmas one year, so they'd start strumming a song and we'd all sing along. They'd take turns to play songs like 'House of the Rising Sun', and everyone would join in. The whole time I'd be getting ready, going over one of the songs I'd learned at home in my head. And then, when it came to my turn, I'd get up and tap my foot and count to three. 'One … two … three', and then I'd start singing the words, a capella. I'd be there with my eyes closed, shaking my head. Maybe the first few times I was a bit nervous, getting up and singing in front of all these people, but I always got a big round of applause and then I'd relax and have fun. Me and my sister and a couple of my cousins would do the 'Macarena' and get everyone to join in. We had so many of those nights over at my nan's and it was those times and practising on that karaoke machine that grew the confidence in me to be able to sing and perform in front of other people.

My mam and my sister Denise and my brother Alan can all play a bit of music too. We had one of those upright pianos in the middle of the conservatory at home for Denise, who was actually the talented one in the house. She was far more musical than I was and she'd later become a qualified music teacher. Denise is incredibly outgoing as well. She's like my nan, the sort of person who walks into a room and everyone notices. She's an entrepreneur and now owns an English language school in Spain, and she's done very well for herself. She also became an awesome piano player and won the Swords 'Young Musician of the Year' when we were still kids. I'd tinker around on that piano, hitting the odd key and listening to the sound it made. I was fascinated by how I could string a few notes together by hitting the keys in the right sequence. I remember my parents came home one day and went mental when they discovered I'd scratched numbers over each of the keys with a butter knife. Because I couldn't read music I'd just go by the sounds. I'd been trying to play this song, I don't know the name of it, but it's from the movie *Big* with Tom Hanks. You know that scene when they do the duet by dancing on the giant keys in the store? It's that one, and a lot of people who learn the piano practise that song. So I had scratched in the numbers 1 and 2 and 3 over the keys so I could remember where my fingers would go.

Under the '1' I'd know if I hit that key it would make that sound. And under the '2' I knew where that sound was. It worked pretty well, until my parents came in and they were like, 'Stephen! What the HELL did you do to the piano? You've ruined it!' But, look, it was an old second-hand one that they'd picked up somewhere, it wasn't one of those expensive Steinways, but they had just paid to have it restored and now there were all these little numbers etched into the paint. And they're still there to this day. I think I was probably sent to my room, but the punishment didn't last long. And when I was allowed near the piano again those little numbers did help me remember where to put my fingers. I kept messing around on it and learning new things. Because I was showing such an interest in the piano my parents decided to send me to the same piano teacher in school that Denise went to, but I didn't enjoy it. It didn't click with me. The teacher was trying to teach me the basics, there were quavers and crotchets, but I just found it all very boring. I was a terrible student because

I couldn't read music and had no interest in learning how to. I think I left after a couple of lessons or maybe he asked me to leave, I can't remember; maybe it was a bit of both. I preferred just to see what I could come up with myself by messing around with the piano, at home. Denise would also show me how to play a few notes, and very slowly I started to pick it up, badly, but that's how I learned, by ear, and with a little help from my sister.

There was also a big old acoustic guitar lying around that my mam had played when she was still in college, and I remember taking it out. She knew a few tunes from playing in pubs and that, not for money but just, ya know, 'Let's have a sing-song' kinda vibe, and I'd take that guitar up to my room and sit there on my bed just strumming it. Physically it was too big for me and I'd have to lay it down horizontally on my lap so I could reach the strings. My brother, who was also learning guitar at the time, showed me how to play 'Everybody Hurts' by R.E.M. It's one of their most powerful songs but it's a simple melody. I loved the way you could do that, listen to a song and then try to replicate it on the guitar.

My parents saw how I was getting more into the guitar than the piano so they probably thought it was worth forking out for a few lessons in that instead. They sent me to the same teacher Alan had been going to, a guy called Gerry Donovan, who used to give classes once a week in the local community centre, and he started teaching me the basics. First, he taught the class how to strum, by playing a simple, traditional song called 'Michael, Row the Boat Ashore'. We'd all sit there and strum down, down, up, down, up, down, down. Then I moved on to playing basic chords, like C and G, A minor and F. Once you get a handle on them, you can play almost any song. And that's probably where my love affair with the guitar really began. It was magical to me, to be able to sit down and string a few chords together and make the same sound as the songs on the records I was listening to at home. I'd spend hours in my bedroom on my own, just strumming the strings, trying to play Elvis songs and 'Johnny B. Goode'.

In primary school I was known as 'the singer', even though I was the one sitting at the back of the class most of the time, hoping the teacher wouldn't ask me any questions. I went to Holy Family Junior National School in Swords, where my mam taught. It was kinda cool having her there, because – and I'm sure they still do this to this day – if a teacher is out sick or whatever then the class gets split up. They'd send all the kids into different classrooms and I'd be allowed to go sit at the back of my mam's class and she wouldn't give me too much work to do. I must have been really young, but I have this random memory of being in the yard at break time and a kid coming up to me and not believing that I didn't live in the school. I don't know why he insisted that I lived there. I think maybe he thought all teachers lived in school and because my mam was teaching there he assumed we both lived there. It's an odd memory alright, but I think that got around and then loads of kids thought I lived there, no matter what I said.

Both our parents were very supportive when we were growing up, in everything we did. My mam stressed the need to have a good education and so did my dad. He was the same as my mam, ya know, he'd be like, 'Ya have to study,' but at the same time he'd be in the background, quietly approving when I showed a serious interest in music.

I didn't engage much in primary school and just did the bare minimum to get through. Most of the time I just put my head down and got on with it and tried not to draw attention to myself. I didn't mind the work so much as having to deal with this constant discomfort and unease I felt around the other kids and the teachers. I don't know why I felt like that. I've gone through a lot of work since then, trying to understand myself and the reasons why I felt the way I did, but sometimes there are no quick and easy answers. All I knew back then was that it was music, again, that would take me out of myself. My teacher in second class, Miss Murphy, had a sort of 'show and tell' every Friday, where you'd have to get up in front of the whole class and perform a little piece. Some kids would tell a story and some would play the recorder, or do a dance. Some of them didn't want to do it, but I was used to performing by now, from doing karaoke and singing at my nan's house. So when it came to my turn I'd walk to the front of the class, close my eyes and sing one of those songs that I had practised at home. I always had a song prepared even though I only knew a couple, so 'Words' would get another outing as well as 'When the Going Gets Tough'. I probably repeated them a good few times and annoyed some of the other kids but Miss Murphy was always very supportive of me singing. She was another one of those people in my life who would be quietly encouraging me. Every time I sang she'd say, 'Ah, you're great, Stephen, that was really, really nice', and that made me feel good about myself too. I kind of enjoyed those Fridays. After being the quiet one all week it was my opportunity to show everyone, ya know, look what I can do. It was one of the few times that I felt comfortable because it was something I knew I could do well. So that had a big impact on my confidence, singing-wise at least.

And I suppose that's how I became known as 'the singer' in school. I'd go on to sing at communions and confirmations in the church. I was still this super-shy, reserved kid but whenever people asked me to sing or perform, even in front of a small crowd, I could do it without even thinking about it. I found it easier to sing, truthfully, than to talk to someone. Talking made me really nervous, but when I'd sing, I would be away.

I was so shy and anxious as a kid that I remember when I was about 11, walking to school and I'd cross the road if I saw anyone I knew coming towards me on the same side. Interacting with people made me nervous so I'd try to avoid them as much as possible. As weird as this sounds now, it wasn't a big deal for me then. I just adopted these little coping strategies, like crossing the road and trying to avoid places where there were too many people, like shopping centres. I'd always just try to keep my head down and maintain a low profile, as much as possible.

But looking back now, I can see how that's a symptom of social anxiety. I didn't know at the time that what I was doing was avoidance, running away from what made me uncomfortable, but this kind of behaviour creates other bad habits such as rumination, overthinking, and in particular, 'all or nothing' thinking. Or catastrophic thinking, where if one thing goes wrong, it makes you think everything has gone wrong. It can really lead you down into a spiral of negative thought patterns and then it just builds up and up until, in my case, it flared into one big panic attack. And even when that happened I ran away from that too. That's the problem with anxiety, you can always try and avoid dealing with whatever it is that makes you anxious, and you get by and everything is fine and it's not an issue, until it gets to a point where you have no choice but to go, 'Okay, this is a problem.'

Maybe my parents sensed this but they never said anything to me at the time. It was years later that my mam told me that they had decided to send me to stage school, when I was about nine, to encourage myself and my sister Fiona to 'come out of our shells a bit', as she described it. This made sense to me at the time because I did love singing but I found it incredibly difficult when I first started going there.

They enrolled us in the Helen Jordan Stage School, which at the time was in the basement of Findlater's Church, on Parnell Square. I remember walking in the first time and there were all these loud kids there, singing and dancing. I just gave my name and immediately sat down quickly at the back and didn't say anything to anyone.

I'd go there with Fiona every Wednesday evening. There were dance classes and there was acting and singing but it took me weeks before I got involved in any of the activities. I'd just sit and watch while all the other kids were going through their routine with the teachers. By their very nature, stage school kids are outgoing and confident and I'd sit there comparing myself to them and feeling even more like the odd one out. I'd be thinking, *I want to be more like them, why can't I be more like that?*, and that, no doubt, added to the feelings that I just wasn't good enough. The stage school people were trying to get me more involved but I didn't like dancing, so I thought I'd try the acting instead. That didn't work either. I just didn't understand the concept. I was like, *Oh, I'm supposed to try and be someone else and get into character.* But I just didn't get it. I remember having to get up in front of all the other kids during the acting lessons and pretend I was someone else. I would be standing there, a big ball of nerves, stuttering and shaking. And then, when I got to sit back down, I'd put my head in my hands and go, 'Oh my God, that was horrible,' and beat myself up. Even if everyone else was saying, 'Well done, well done,' I'd still be curling up inside.

And that's very revealing to me now because that's what I did, all the time. I'd beat myself up horribly. It was a habit I got into. If I felt that something didn't go right, I'd be relentlessly hard on myself.

But I kept going, every week, because I knew, deep down, that if I ever got the opportunity to sing, I could show them what I could do. But I never did get the chance because I never put myself out there. I found myself just being one of the backing singers. Sometimes, like at the end of the year, the stage school would put on a show in the Olympia on Dame Street or wherever and myself and Fiona would get to go along. There's a picture of both of us, about nine or ten, and we're all dressed up. I think that was taken at one of those shows. I remember being on stage singing, with 50 or 60 kids, but I'd stand right at the back behind all of them.

Now and again, some of the other kids would audition for different roles that came up and lots of them were getting awesome parts in big musicals or dramas, and I felt even more left out. But then my mam got a call, I think from a friend of the woman who ran the stage school, saying they needed someone for something to do with Pokémon, which was huge back then. For some reason, they asked me. I don't know why, maybe they felt sorry for me because I wasn't getting anything else, but I was excited. Pokémon was massive, every kid loved Pokémon and I was a big fan and had Pokémon cards and the game and everything. I was like, *Oh my God, I'm going to be in something to do with Pokémon*, and I couldn't wait to find out what it was all about. We went in my dad's car to some town, where I realised I had to dress up in a bright yellow Pikachu costume and walk in the local parade. I was a bit tubby at the time so I fit the bill. So there I was, barely able to breathe, wobbling off down the road in this feckin' giant Pikachu costume with all these other people dressed as Pokémon characters. It was really hot and uncomfortable in there and I was sweating. My dad said to me years later that he felt really sorry for me because he saw me struggling and trying not to fall over. It wasn't the most glamorous start to my performing career but it was my first paid gig and I got 50 quid for it, which was a lot of money for a kid back then.

You know, going to stage school exposed all my insecurities and brought them to the surface, but it would ultimately help me with my confidence and I've a lot of appreciation now for the opportunities that came through it. I couldn't act and I couldn't dance but I did start putting myself out there a bit more. Now, while I was never going to be an actor and never even wanted to be one, I did go for a few auditions for some small roles that came up. There was one I did, when I was about ten years of age, for the director Jim Sheridan's daughter Kirsten, out in their big house on the southside. I can't remember what it was for but there were all these other kids going for an audition. I sat there listening while they gave me the gist of the character they wanted me to play but I didn't understand what they were asking me to do, and I didn't get the part.

But I did get to be an extra on *Fair City*, the RTÉ soap, when I was still about ten. It was through the stage school and some of the boys were picked to be part of a football team and I was one of them. I remember going into RTÉ for the very first time and going into the canteen, somewhere I've been many times since, and sitting down and getting free lunch, you know. It was pretty exciting.

And then we went outside and they had cameras filming us as we ran around kicking the ball on the grass. We hung out for the whole day and we got paid for it, like 40 or 50 quid. And then it was on TV but it was a 'blink and you missed it' moment. I think I was there for like a split second in the background.

That did lead on to getting a part in the movie *Agnes Brown* that was based on a book by the comedian Brendan O'Carroll, when I was 11. I think most of the kids in the stage school were extras of some sort in *Agnes Brown* and my sister Fiona was in some of the scenes too.

It was shot out in Bray, I think, and they had this whole movie set there. It was like a mock seaside village with a Punch and Judy box and everything. We were in the background walking along the seafront. It was on TV there a little while ago and my sister sent me a clip of it and we were like, 'Oh look, there we are,' but yeah, it was another very, very brief moment.

It was still exciting to be on TV as a kid and I suppose that's really when the stage school did start helping me to come out of my shell.

I started doing these little talent shows that used to be on in towns and villages all over Ireland. If you were a kid then, you could enter your local talent show and maybe even win a prize. I vaguely remember doing one in Dundalk when I was about 10, and I think that was the first one I ever did. We all travelled up in the car, and in the show I sang 'Unchained Melody' by The Righteous Brothers. I remember there was also a group of teenagers there and one was dressed as Britney Spears and they were doing that song 'Hit Me Baby One More Time', with all the backing singers in matching outfits lip-syncing. There were a few other acts as well and they were all pretty good. I didn't get anywhere but they did give me a certificate for taking part. I remember coming off stage and feeling the same way I had that time in Courtown. There were people clapping and cheering and it felt really good. It was a boost to my confidence and it made me think, *Okay, this is cool, maybe I am good*, you know?

I really enjoyed it and after that I got well and truly into doing these talent shows whenever there was one on. Now, don't get me wrong, I would still be incredibly nervous. Like, before I sang, I'd have to introduce myself and say, 'Hello, I'm Stephen Garrigan, from Swords,' and I'd be so nervous that my words would be all shaky. For me, those first few moments on stage were the worst. But then, as soon as I started singing, I was grand. Now I was looking for any excuse to go and get up on stage.

My mam has this scrapbook and it's mad when I look through it. In among all these family holiday photos are clippings from newspapers of different things I was doing in the stage school from around that time. There's one clipping of me and Fiona in an article in the local newspaper, titled 'Swords Brother, Sister in Talent Finals'. That was a competition in Pontins in Prestatyn. It was kinda like a Butlin's but in Wales. Myself and Fiona had entered a talent show here, in Mosney, and I came joint first with the Irish boy who was later in the Harry Potter movies, Devon Murray. He was dressed up as the Artful Dodger and he was doing the 'Consider Yourself' song from *Oliver!* while I was singing 'My Heart Will Go On' by Celine Dion. It was from the movie *Titanic* that had come out that year and it was this massive hit. It was absolutely everywhere and I kinda picked it up because it was on the radio all the time. All these family parks would host a talent show and the winners then got to go to this big final. We didn't win but the whole family got a free trip over to Wales and my parents were delighted.

From doing these talent shows my confidence grew and

I started getting more involved in stage school. It mentions in that article that I was in the middle of recording a song for National Children's Day. It was for charity and the stage school put together a little group of me and four girls to record a cover of the Eurythmics song 'Sisters Are Doing it for Themselves' that was called 'Children Are Doing it for Themselves'. The idea was to get all the kids in Ireland to buy it and make it number 1. And then all the money would go to these charities and children's hospitals. We recorded it in a studio and I remember it was very brief. We just went in and sang a couple of lines from the song. I had to stand behind the mic and sing my bit and then it was over. But when the single did come out we went on a little tour around the country.

It was utterly bizarre to me at the time, going around on a bus and getting up on these makeshift stages that would be set up in all these shopping centres. Every weekend we'd go off to some other part of the country, to Cork, or Offaly, and then me and the girls would sing the song along with all these backing dancers. We did a few in Dublin as well, including a performance at the Ideal Homes Exhibition in the RDS.

We even got to go on *The Late Late Show*, Ireland's biggest talk show, where we performed in front of a live audience in the RTÉ studios. I think my parents enjoyed that more than I did because they got to hang out in the green room and meet the presenter, Pat Kenny. But by this stage we must have done the same routine dozens of times and I was getting used to it. When you're in stage school with all these other kids dancing and singing, after a while it just becomes the norm. But it was a really great way to gain confidence and experience.

There's another newspaper article with a picture of me with four other lads in Boyzonly – 'the world's youngest tribute band'. We were part of a panto, *Sleeping Beauty*, that was on in St Anthony's Theatre on Merchant's Quay around Christmas 1999.

My grandad lived in Santry in north Dublin, next door to Alan Hughes, the TV guy, who was one of the producers of the panto. And my grandad had decided, unbeknownst to me, to give Alan a tape recording of me singing 'My Heart Will Go On' at the talent show in the UK. My grandad knew Alan had a panto coming up and he thought I was a pretty good singer so he dropped this tape in, just to see what would come out of it. Alan must have liked it because we got a call from him asking me did I want to come in and audition for the part of Ronan Keating, the lead singer of Boyzone, who were huge at the time. I got the gig and was paired off with four other lads for our different roles. We all dressed up like each of the members of Boyzone, in our white suits and all, and I wore the same round glasses that Ronan did. We had it down to a tee. We did songs like 'When the Going Gets Tough', which I knew well, 'No Matter What', which was a big hit for Boyzone at the time and their cover of Tracy Chapman's 'Baby Can I Hold You'.

One of the kids in Boyzonly was Johnny Ward, who would go on to do loads of stage stuff and TV. Johnny was much more outgoing than me. He was that typical stage school kid, cool and confident and very talented, while I was still the shy one in the corner, but it was good experience, I suppose, in the hard graft of working and performing. We would do two shows a day, a matinée and one in the evening, and we did some short interviews as well, on breakfast TV and, I remember, *The Den*, which was every kid's favourite show back then. We'd do a few rehearsals and then go on stage. I loved the singing and performing, but offstage I'd just fall back into myself. I'd just kind of sit there and be really, really quiet.

I also remember auditioning for a part in *Les Misérables*, which was going to be on in the Point Theatre, and there were rounds and rounds of auditions over three days. I was still there on the last day and I remember thinking, *Holy shit, I might have this*, but then when it got down to the last few kids I was sent outside the room and I suddenly realised that I hadn't got it. I didn't appreciate it then, just how well I'd done to get down to the last few out of hundreds, which is amazing, but I'd thought I really had it and I was gutted. But what was even more devastating was finding out later that it was because I was a little bit overweight. I was going for the part of Gavroche, and I suppose it makes sense that I didn't get it because this character is a skinny little street urchin. I don't know if it was said to me, or if I overheard, but it was heartbreaking and I remember crying about it with my dad.

When I look back at pictures of my time in stage school now, it makes me cringe a little bit and sometimes I think, *What was I doing?* Because once the band started off and I was getting into all that, I swept all of this under the carpet and tried to forget about it. Years later it just didn't seem to be cool to be talking about being in stage school and I was a bit embarrassed by it. But for me, back then, it was an outlet for a very shy kid.

My family thought this was great fun, and while my parents were very encouraging, they didn't take it too seriously. The likelihood, at this stage, of me making anything out of myself, through music or performing, would have been very slim. There was no conversation at home about me doing this for a living. It was just a fun kid thing to do. Like, even my grandad, even though he had sent that tape in to Alan Hughes, would have been very much of that traditional Irish mentality of 'do well in school, get a decent job and do a solid day's work'. He left school at 12 and worked on the family farm, and at 19 he got a job and he stayed at the same job for the rest of his life. But apparently he was proud of me being on TV.

I remember we did one of the breakfast shows, like *Ireland AM*, where we performed our little routine. I think we sang 'No Matter What', and at the end of it the presenter came over and asked us a few questions. When it came to my turn, he asked me what would I like to be when I grew up and I answered, 'A singer.' I just said that because I couldn't think of anything else to say.

Afterwards we looked back at a recording of the show with my grandparents, and my grandad couldn't hear it properly. When I said, 'A singer' in answer to the presenter's question, Grandad turned to me and said, 'What did you say you wanted to be? A fireman? Aah, good lad, good lad, you'd make a great fireman.' I started laughing and then he said, 'Or a garda. You'd be a great garda.'

2

THE ROAD THAT I GREW UP ON was part of a big housing estate called River Valley, just outside the town of Swords in North Dublin. Most of the roads in the estate had houses on both sides, facing each other, but on our road the houses just faced across into the valley. All the kids in that part of the estate were super close, and most of those I grew up with on that road remain some of my closest friends to this day. There was John and Matt, they were a few houses down; Paul, who was over in my house last Christmas; and Andy Lowry, who lives in Maastricht now, he used to live two doors down and he was one of my best friends growing up. There's actually a picture of the two of us somewhere, we're about two years old and we're sitting in a cot. I think he's dressed as a sailor, for some reason.

We'd all play out in the green area in front of my house and most days after school we'd kick footballs around 'til all hours. Everybody would join in – my dad, Alan, some of Alan's mates and some of the other neighbours. We'd make teams and that just became a regular thing, particularly at weekends. From that, it was a natural thing to join the local football club, and I started playing for River Valley Rangers at the age of eight. Outside of going to stage school, I'd train during the week with the team, and then play every Sunday. I was a defender and I was half decent. Like, I played for a while on the B team and now and again I'd play a couple of matches in the premier division where a few of those players would have gone on to play for Ireland. I continued playing 'til I was about 14 but by then I was studying hard for my Junior Cert in secondary school and I never really went back. I still play now, five-a-side, with mates – well, I did pre-Covid – 'cause it's good, you know, it's a bit of craic.

Through football I got to know this kid called Neale, who was also on the team. Through his cheekiness and gift of the gab he would talk his way into becoming our first band manager when we started out as 21 Demands. He would later become the stage tech for Kodaline, looking after the guitars and the amps and making sure everything was working properly. And now he's the tour manager for the band, and has been all over the world with us. But his first ever job was as my 'amp engineer' and I'll tell you about that in a bit.

I started secondary school in September 2001, aged 13. I was going to Coláiste Choilm in Swords, or 'The Bros' as we called it, because it was run by the Christian Brothers. It's still known as 'The Bros' to anyone who has ever gone there. My dad went to the same school in the 1960s, when it first opened. It was a big step up for me from primary school. While a few of the lads I knew from Holy Family also went to 'The Bros', what happens is, you're separated and put into different classes.

Most of the friends I had made in primary school ended up in different classes, so I felt a little bit like, *Oh shit, I don't know anybody here.* I was fairly sure most of the kids felt that way.

But because I was so shy it wasn't like I was able to go up to groups of lads and go, 'Hey, what's your name?' and make new friends. I just, again, sort of kept myself to myself, but one of the first people I did start talking to in my class was a lad called Brendan. I think the only reason I was able to speak to him in the first place was because his older brother was in my older brother's class, so that was my in. I was put sitting beside him, and then I built up the confidence one day to say, 'Hey, your brother knows my brother' and then we just kinda started hanging out with each other. And Bren is still one of my best friends to this day. I also hooked up with Neale and they became the two lads I mainly hung out with in first year.

When I first went into 'The Bros' I remember thinking, *Okay, primary school is over, now it's time to knuckle down.* So for the first year my main focus was on education and studying for my Junior Cert. I became a bit of a study freak and I took it seriously.

My family is very college-orientated and for my parents, education is very important. Even later, when I was trying to get my foot in the door of the music industry my parents would be like, 'Okay, but make sure you have a backup plan, so stay in college and get your education.' Which is fair enough.

But at this point, singing and performing and all that was still just a fun hobby and there was no reason whatsoever to think it would be anything other than that. There was never a point at that stage that it occurred to me, you know, 'I'm going to make a career out of this.'

And my parents, being parents, were right, in a way, telling me to work hard and get my Junior Certificate and get my Leaving Certificate and get into college, so that's what I aimed for.

I wasn't a really good student and I wasn't a particularly bad one either. I was somewhere in the middle but I did work hard. I would always have my homework done and I was a very well-behaved, quiet student (and I hope my teachers would agree with me!).

I got some good grades in first year but that wasn't because I particularly liked school or liked studying. I got through the first year exams, though I think I got a D in something and I remember feeling pretty shit about it.

For some reason I thought I wanted to get into law. I don't know where that idea came from. I was watching a movie – I think it might have been a courtroom drama or something like that – and there was a lawyer in it who was very outspoken and confident. As I watched it, I think part of me realised that I would like to be more like that. I mentioned it to my parents, and then once I had said it, it kinda stuck and I felt like I had to do it. I knew that, in order to do law, I'd have to focus in school, and at the same time my parents were also stressing the importance of working hard, so yeah, I felt a certain amount of pressure. But I was never going to be a lawyer, that was not going to be the right fit for me. It just sounded like a good job, so I thought I'd go for it; it was as random as that.

All through these early teenage years I think I was alright, even though I was still this incredibly shy person. I was only really comfortable around people I knew, like Bren. I found it hard to make other friends because when I met new people I'd still be very nervous around them. In class, if I was asked to speak I would feel incredibly anxious. I'd do what I did in primary school, you know, sit quietly at the back, not put my hand up for anything and think, *Please don't ask me, please don't ask me.*

That's probably not that unusual for most teenagers, who can be a bit unsure of themselves, but I was still doing the same things I had been doing when I was younger, like crossing the road to avoid people. When I was with my friends I found some level of comfort but whenever I was on my own around strangers I'd immediately feel anxious. I'd keep my head down, not wanting to draw any attention to myself and I'd try to avoid conversations, if at all possible.

To be honest, it wasn't really an issue for me, I just accepted it. I was happy enough, just sitting quietly in the corner, and while sometimes I'd wish I was more outgoing or one of the more popular kids, it wasn't something I worried about. But looking back on it now, this shyness, this discomfort around other people, while it was okay by me at the time, when I got older it would turn into something way more debilitating. This was the anxiety I had first felt as a kid and as time went by it was continuing to build up.

So, outside of Bren and Neale I did find it hard to make new friends in school, but then when I started to skateboard, I found all these other guys who had skateboards, and that's when I started to make new friends. There was Brian and Paul who were also in my class. I bonded with them over skateboarding and we'd all hang around together at lunch break.

I was playing Tony Hawk's *Pro Skater* video game, which was absolutely massive back then. I was obsessed with that game, everybody was. Everyone was playing it on their games consoles and then you'd look out the window and all the kids would be out on the road doing tricks and jumps with their new skateboards. I loved that game so much that I figured I'd like to go out and try to do it for real.

For a birthday, I think it was, my parents got me one. In fairness to my parents, they were always pretty awesome because if you were interested in something they'd always support it, though my dad was constantly effing and blinding about the skateboard. He was wary of them and he'd be like, 'Make sure you don't break anything or fall off,' but that didn't stop me jumping over big gaps in walls and doing tricks on it. I got pretty good at it too, and then I started hanging around at the back of the old Superquinn supermarket in Swords, where all the other skater kids gathered.

Every Wednesday we had a half day in school, so I'd go down there, sometimes with Neale, and we'd hang out and show off our skills. It was a perfect spot for skateboarding because the ground was very smooth so we could fly up and down and all the skaters would take turns doing tricks and that. Different gangs of lads would gather there and it became a kind of little community in itself. I felt comfortable with them because we all had this common interest. There was a bond there too, because I think skateboarders are typically misfits in a way and they have their own dress sense and lingo. I didn't really dress like them but for me it was a group I felt I belonged to. You know in school how there's different cliques? Well, for me, I suppose the skaters felt like a clique that I could feel part of. But it wasn't just that, I genuinely loved skating, and then when I found other people who also loved it, it was awesome, like a whole new, cool world had revealed itself to me.

So I'd work real hard all week so I could be free that Wednesday afternoon to take a break from studying and go skateboarding. There could be like, 20 to 30 lads there, all in different groups, and I started to meet and hang around and get to know some of them.

I was still going to stage school for the first few months of first year but I had kept that quiet. I was in a new school, with new people, and I didn't want to be known as 'the singer' anymore. I was a teenager now and being a singer and dancing with kids in a stage school just didn't seem that cool. I've nothing against stage schools and I'm still very appreciative of the opportunities that it gave me, but even when you say 'stage school' I think you have this idea of kids singing and dancing and smiles and cheesy stuff. And I was in an all-boys school now, and I was conscious that other guys there would rip it out of you, if they had an excuse. There's always a bit of slagging going on among lads and I wanted to avoid getting stick over it. I was still going every Wednesday evening, for the first half of first year, but it had become more and more boring. I was never going to be an actor, and dancing just made me uncomfortable. I'm still no dancer to this day. I think Fiona felt the same as me. She kinda grew out of it too and wasn't really bothered either.

All I ever wanted to do as a kid was sing, but I'd been going to Gerry, the guitar teacher, while I was still in primary school, and by the time I was in first year I was getting pretty good. Now I knew what I wanted to do. I wanted to play guitar, and sing. I didn't want to be in stage school anymore. It just didn't fit me and I was getting more and more uncomfortable going there, so half way through first year, I quietly dropped out.

Instead, every Monday night I'd go down to the community centre, literally a five-minute walk from my house, for lessons, with my brother Alan's guitar that I had borrowed strapped on my back.

Gerry was a fairly well-known local musician. He was in a band too, and I think they released some songs and a charity single. He was actually a bass player in the band but he'd also sing on his own, in the local pubs around Swords, and he still does. He'd also go away every summer as well, to play in the pubs and clubs in Spain for the tourist season.

He was a good teacher and what set him apart was that he showed a genuine interest in the people who came to him. Like, he would teach everybody in the class and then each person would get a bit of one-to-one time with him too.

After class I'd go home, go up to my bedroom, close the door and mess around on the guitar for hours on my own. And that's how I spent most of my free time in the evenings. I started progressing quite fast and after about a year I had moved into the advanced class.

Anyone who was learning guitar at the time went to Gerry. My brother had also been going to him for lessons but when I was still in beginners Alan was already in advanced, and he left not long after I started. My sister Denise went to Gerry too and it's where I got to know Phil Magee. I think it's fair to say that if it wasn't for Phil, there would be no Kodaline. He was from the same place as me, River Valley, and now he's a big music producer in Ireland. He's worked as a producer with The Script and loads of other acts and he's still one of my best friends today.

This is crazy, right. Phil was born on the same day as my older brother and my mam and his mam were next to each other in the same ward in the same hospital. Phil became quite pally with my older brother when they were super young, and I vaguely remember him being in the house. But when I got to know him, through going to Gerry's, I was still very young myself, probably only around 13. Phil was in one of Gerry's more advanced classes and he was in a band himself at the time. Phil left school at 15 to become a sound engineer and ended up working in a recording studio in town. He would later become a judge at the Battle of the Bands in 'The Bros' and when we won it one year he took us into the studio when we were still like, 16, for our first recording session. From that point onwards we've been close and I still talk to him pretty much every other day.

There were other guys in the guitar class who I'd also meet as time went on, because they'd all be in different bands and we'd compete in various Battle of the Bands competitions. But little did myself and Phil know when we first met that years later we would be in a studio together recording the songs that would make up Kodaline's first album. I'd even go on to write a song for him called 'The One', as a wedding present when he got married.

There was a big talent contest on at the time, in Brackenstown in Swords, not far from where I lived, and in the lead-up to the show Phil was looking for a guitar player. Somebody had said, 'Hey, have you heard this guy?', meaning me, because I had been doing pretty well, but I was a bit too young for them. And then they found another lead guitarist, a guy who was far, far better than me and older, and he ended up getting Phil's band to the final of that show.

Alan and some of his friends had got together and they were going to enter the Brackenstown competition as well. They had started meeting in our house before I went into first year and a lot of that summer I spent listening to them jamming in the sitting room.

My parents didn't allow it all the time, for obvious reasons, because the lads would come in and take over the sitting room and start making very loud music, or noise, depending on who was listening. So they took it in turns to go to each other's houses. It wasn't a band as such, I don't think they even had a name, it was just a few mates who'd come over for a bit of a jam and a laugh. There was a drummer, a guy called

Fabio, who was also in 'The Bros', and Jono, a rhythm guitarist from River Valley who was in my brother's class. The other member, if you like, was Colm Maloney, who lived down the road. I remember Colm well. Before the jamming sessions he'd be calling into the house for my brother and while he was a bit older than me, we got on really well.

They weren't bad either. I remember Colm, in particular, was very talented and he wrote his own riff that I still have in my head that was just class. Now and again, I'd sneak in and pick up one of the electric guitars they had, to mess around with, but they didn't really take me too seriously. I was just the annoying younger brother getting in the way, but I remember being there in the sitting room, listening to them and thinking, *Holy shit, this is so cool, I'd love to be in a band.* And that's probably where the whole idea of being in a band came from, for me.

They were playing a bit of Thin Lizzy and stuff like that, and that's how I got introduced to the *Live and Dangerous* album, which I became obsessed with. I remember them playing 'Jailbreak', which is a classic Thin Lizzy tune, but they were also rocking out 'Hotel California' by the Eagles and trying some Rory Gallagher.

But it was the guitar solos from all these classic rock tracks that grabbed me, and this led to me really, really wanting to get an electric. From watching my brother and his friends jam I started getting into all these great legends of Irish guitar, you know, like Scott Gorham, Rory Gallagher and Gary Moore. I became a huge fan of Thin Lizzy because of Scott Gorham.

When I first started going to Gerry, while I was still in primary school, I'd borrow my brother Alan's acoustic guitar. My mam didn't want me using hers, which is fair enough because she knew I'd probably wreck it, and anyway it was too big.

Alan's guitar was smaller, a three-quarter size one. So I'd be borrowing it all the time but then he'd come in and say, 'Hey, I want to use it,' and I'd have to reluctantly hand it over. I didn't really have a choice, he was bigger than me.

But when he got an electric guitar, I wanted one as well. My dad ended up getting us both these electric guitar starter kits that came with little amps and all. They were pretty nice guitars. Alan had a Fender Squier that my dad had got for him in Argos and from the Waltons music shop in town I got an Epiphone Les Paul, which was awesome because this opened up a whole new world to me.

You can only do so much with an acoustic. Like, they're great for learning on, and years later I'd revert back to using one when I was writing songs, but with an electric I really got into playing guitar solos. With that distortion effect through the amp I could get closer to the sound that all those great guitar legends made. I'd be listening to all these albums in my bedroom and I was obsessed. I'd be playing these songs over and over again until I could do them fluidly, without stopping or making mistakes. And then I instinctively started singing along as I played, and after hours and hours of practice I was able to sing without looking down at my fingers. And I was also starting to put my own little bits and pieces together, trying out a few riffs and chord sequences that I liked. Any chance we got, Alan and myself would be playing our electrics. He'd be playing his and I'd be playing mine, and sometimes we played together, and it was pretty much all day, every day.

Then I'd go to Gerry in guitar class and ask him to show me how to play a song I'd been trying to learn at home. He'd show me the chord sequence and then I'd practise it over and over until I got it right. Every week I'd find something new I wanted to play. One of the first songs I learned was 'Johnny B. Goode', of course, and then I remember asking him to show me how to play the solo from Guns N' Roses' 'Sweet Child O' Mine', which is quite complicated, and 'Tears in Heaven' by Eric Clapton, which took me a while to get, but mostly it was Thin Lizzy stuff. The hardest one for me to grasp was probably 'Emerald'. It's got like this duelling guitar part – well, pretty much the whole song is made up of guitar solos and riffs – and I remember trying to play each part.

I went into the advanced guitar class very, very quickly, like within a year, and I was getting more and more confident. With the big talent show coming up I decided to enter. I remember telling Gerry I was going to do Brackenstown, and he was like, 'Yeah, you should. It will be a great experience.' I couldn't do a guitar solo on my own, without a band, so I thought about playing one of the quieter ballads I had learned on the acoustic. I decided on 'Unchained Melody' by The Righteous Brothers. I was already able to play most of the guitar part and I knew the lyrics too. When I played it for Gerry he was like, 'Oh, I didn't know you were a singer. Yeah, play it just like that.'

I would stop going to Gerry when I was 14, and one of the last things I learned from him was how to play 'Emerald'. It's quite complicated for a young guitar player to learn but I had got it down pretty well. I think it was at that point that Gerry said to me, 'You know what? You got it, Stephen. Just keep improving yourself. I can only take you so far,' and we parted ways.

Years later, in 2015, Kodaline was playing a huge gig in Dublin, in Kilmainham, where we performed to 15,000 people. Gerry had also taught Mark, Kodaline's guitarist, how to play, after I had suggested to Mark that he go to him for lessons. So we invited Gerry up on stage to jam with us. We gave him this top-of-the-range Fender Stratocaster guitar to play and after the song was over we said to him, 'Here, flip it over,' and on the back we had inscribed 'To Gerry, from Stephen and Mark ... Thanks for everything'. He still gigs around Dublin and now and again he'll use that guitar and apparently he shows people the inscription and tells them the lads from Kodaline gave it to him.

The Brackenstown Talent Contest was one of the bigger talent competitions on at that time. Every year towns and villages across Ireland would organise their own talent shows, and singers, musicians, jugglers and magicians from all over the area would take part. They used to be a big deal, and some of them, like Brackenstown, had serious prizes for the winners.

I'm not sure that many of them are still going anymore, which is a shame because I think they're a great opportunity for anybody keen to get into music or who might just want to perform – a few songs maybe, their own or covers – in front of their community. Loads of local people who were just starting out would have been in the Brackenstown Talent Contest.

One guy from Swords, Dave Gilna, I remember, had a comedy act with his friend and he would go on to be a playwright. There was also a girl called Lesley Roy, from Balbriggan, and she represented Ireland in the Eurovision. I remember seeing her at one of these talent shows and thinking, *Holy shit, she can sing.* For me, even though I was still this shy, retiring kid, I loved music, and those talent shows would give me the chance to go do something I really enjoyed. There's only so much you can do on your own, singing and playing guitar, before you have to go and put it out there. And while getting up on stage was daunting, and still is, this was a great way to learn how to deal with the nerves. Through doing these shows, and winning and losing, I got better. It's like anything else: the more you do something, the more comfortable you become at it.

Brackenstown would usually be advertised in one of the local newspapers, the *Fingal Independent* or the *North County Leader*. I think there was an entry fee but it wasn't much, and there was a top prize of around 1,000 euro for the eventual winner. I wasn't really interested in the money, though. This time I wasn't going into a competition as a kid from a stage school, singing a song. Brackenstown would be the first time I'd be playing guitar and singing at the same time. It was something I'd never done before and it was exciting.

The whole competition was run over a number of heats. I think there was one every week for a month and then the following month there'd be the quarter-finals and then the semi-finals and then the final. There was a school there, by the church in Brackenstown, and the first heats were on in the hall. Brackenstown is directly across from where we lived but when we were younger it was like a different part of the world. River Valley is here, and then when you go down the valley and up the steps you're in Brackenstown. There was always like this weird tension between the kids, particularly the teenagers on both sides of the valley. You could be confronted by a gang from Brackenstown if they caught you on their turf, and they'd threaten you with 'Are you from the valley?' There were times when they'd gather on either side and shout insults and slag each other off. The Brackenstown boys would be shouting, 'Yiz better not come into the manor.' I didn't get involved but there was a big rivalry there. They had their own football team as well. I would have played them a few times when I was with River Valley Rangers and it was extra rough with a few dodgy tackles going in and elbows. So there I was years later going over into enemy territory, as it were, for the first heat.

I remember walking into this big hall with my parents and Alan's acoustic guitar on my back. There were loads of chairs laid out, with a stage at the back. There was a lady sitting behind a desk and people had to pay two euro or something like that for a ticket and that also got you into the raffle that would be held at the end. I went in and told the lady I was performing and she gave me a sticker with my name on it. Nervously I went to the backstage area, which was really just one of the rooms off to the side where all the other performers were hanging out, warming up before the show. There were all sorts of different acts in there: there was a magician who was also a juggler, and loads of musicians and a lot of other singers. There were young kids singing along to backing tracks and stuff like that and everybody was kind of going through their routines. The juggler was throwing things up in the air and the guitarists were tuning up their instruments while the singers were going through their scales, 'do re mi fa so la ti do'.

There were all ages there but I think most of them would still have been kids. The oldest was probably around 18. At 13, I was one of the youngest. Nervously I said hello and then kept my head down, being my usual shy self.

As the compère was going around getting everyone's names and organising the running order I remember thinking, *Please don't let me go on first, please don't let me go on first.* I had come to the conclusion pretty quickly that going on first was going to be tough, because everybody was still in the hall taking their seats and talking and chatting. If you were going on first you would have to win the crowd over while they were all distracted. In the end I was chosen to go on third, which I was still a little bit worried about because I thought it was a bit too soon. I think you only had to play one song in the first heat and then in the later heats you played two. I was working it out in my head. Each act was only going to be on stage for about five minutes, max. Some would go over but, with two acts ahead of me, that still gave me a little while before it was my turn. I was thinking at least I was on in the first half and not the second, when I would have had to wait over an hour because it would be after the intermission, when people started milling around again. I didn't want to be waiting that long. But as it got closer to show time I started to get really anxious. I wanted to go on and get it over with but I didn't want to go on, at the same time.

When I found out I was to be third I sat back down with my parents in the audience to watch the first act. They had bought a programme for the show and my name was on it. It said, 'Stephen Garrigan. Singing. And playing guitar'. I thought that was funny, 'Singing. And playing guitar'. I don't know why. I think it was just the nerves.

Then I went back and stood at the side of the stage waiting for my turn. I remember being so nervous that there were butterflies in my stomach. I was taking deep breaths and trying to keep my composure. The second act finished and then the compère, as he was going back on stage, gestured at me with his hand to get ready. Then he said, 'Ladies and gentlemen, wasn't she great? Wasn't she great? Okay, and now, here we have young Stephen Garrigan from River Valley and he'll be singing and playing 'Unchained Melody' for us tonight. Let's give him a great big round of applause.'

And then, I was on. I have a clip of it on my phone. Even though it's really bad quality, you can almost see how nervous I am. You can even hear the compère asking everyone to quieten down: 'He's a little nervous,' he says. I think that paints a good picture of what it was like for me. A deer caught in the headlights comes to mind.

I walked over and stood under the spotlight. I looked up and there was the audience in front of me. This was a big hall and it was packed. In the first heats there could have been as many as 16 different acts, so all their families were there, my parents were there, waving up, my neighbours were there, people from all over, and in front of them were the judges, sitting at a table, looking right up at me.

I strummed the first couple of chords – and then everybody started talking. This seemed to happen to me a lot when I was younger. I'd go on stage and introduce myself. At first it would quieten down, and then I'd go up to the mic and say, nervously, 'Ahem, I'm ... eh ... Stephen, and ... eh ... I'm going to do a song,' and everyone would start talking. The compère would have to come back out on stage and say, 'Will you give him a bit of quiet here, you know, he's very nervous.' It happened pretty much every single time.

So I closed my eyes and started singing the words. Now, I was probably singing it a bit too high as my voice still hadn't broken, but either because the compère told them to shut up or because they genuinely liked it, I don't know, suddenly everything went quiet. I kept my eyes closed the whole time and then, just like that, there was a huge round of applause and the compère was back on. 'Wasn't he great, ladies and gentlemen, wasn't he just great.' I opened my eyes. People were cheering and clapping. I felt a massive wave of relief.

The whole time I was on stage singing I was away in a different space and the nerves only hit me before and after I was performing. I went back down on wobbly legs to sit with my parents to watch the rest of the show.

'You were brilliant, Stephen, absolutely brilliant,' they were saying, but I just remember thinking the whole time, *I hope I get through, I hope I get through.* I was dreading the judging part in case my name wasn't called out.

I sat watching the other acts, trying to distract myself but not really paying attention, until the intermission. I can't even remember the second half, and then it was decision time. This was the most stressful part, when all the acts were finished and the judges went off to a back room just outside the hall. I remember waiting for them to come back in with the names of the people who had got through and those that hadn't. I was so freakin' nervous. I was thinking, *What if I don't get through, what do I do then?*

Because in my head I was like, *Okay, I can try again next year but wait, that's another year! What am I going to do for the rest of the year?* All these thoughts were jumbling through my mind. As difficult as this first show was for me, I was still aware that there were not a lot of opportunities back then to get in front of an audience and perform, especially at my age.

Then the judges came back in. I think in the early heats half of the acts would make it through and half wouldn't. So they started by calling out the names of those who didn't and wishing them better luck next time, you know, asking them to please come back, because they didn't want to discourage people and shatter anybody's dreams. And then they announced who would go through … and I was one of them. I was so relieved. I remember going home with my mam and dad and we were all delighted. But then I had to wait until the next round so I spent as much time as I could practising.

For the next round I asked Neale to come along with me and he was like, 'Yeah, why not? It'll be a bit of craic.' This time I had brought along a little amp so I could plug it into the guitar to make it sound better, and I asked Neale to carry it in for me. When we got to the desk where they sold the tickets the lady gave me my little sticker with my name on it. Then she turned around to Neale and asked him, 'And what do you do?'

Quick as a flash, he said, 'Oh, I'm the amp engineer,' as he stood there with the amp in his hand.

She didn't know any better, so she gave him a sticker with 'Amp Engineer' written on it. He was laughing because he got away with not paying the two euro entry fee. Now, Neale knew nothing about amps, and half way through my performance, didn't the amp blow up. I was strumming and strumming but there was no sound. I remember turning to side stage to look for him but he was nowhere to be seen. I'm like, 'Neale! Neale!' in a loud stage whisper, but he was gone. The compère came back on and told the audience, 'Sorry, sorry, we have a problem here,' and everyone had to wait while I borrowed someone else's amp and plugged it in. I managed to finish the song, and somehow I got through to the semi-final. After the show, Neale reappeared, but without his 'Amp Engineer' badge that he had sheepishly taken off and thrown away. I still find it hilarious that Neale, my 'amp engineer' that night, would later become the tour manager for Kodaline. He would go on to work for Coca-Cola but when we got our first record deal we said to him, 'Here, just come on the road with us, you can be our guitar tech.' And he did. To this day, we still laugh about the night he was the amp engineer.

In the meantime, my brother's band, who had ended up calling themselves Róisín Dubh after the Thin Lizzy song, was in one of the other heats. They played a lot of Thin Lizzy with a bit of 'Hotel California' by the Eagles thrown in and I remember watching them and thinking they were amazing. But they didn't get through. I couldn't believe it, I thought they were robbed. But I think I was more disappointed than they were. Like, they weren't really that fazed. But one thing that stands out is that Jono in the band, one of my brother's mates, had this unbelievable guitar, an Ovation that his dad had lent him for the show.

It's an acoustic guitar, and it's got this round plastic back and they're very rare and very, very expensive. After Róisín Dubh got knocked out, Jono's dad let me use his Ovation for the semi-final, which was unbelievable. I remember being backstage and Jono's dad saying, 'Do you want to use my guitar?' He was looking at the one I had, which was all bashed up and a bit shit. And I was like, 'Are you serious?'

Steve Garrigan

I was shitting it in case I broke it but it gave me a big boost of confidence going into the semi-final. I was thinking I must be doing something right, if he was willing to trust me with it.

For the semi-finals each musical act had to do two songs, so as well as 'Unchained Melody', I did a medley of 'Brown Eyed Girl' and 'Knockin' On Heaven's Door' that I had been practising. I had learned that both these classics had similar chords so I was able to mesh them together at home. I was fairly confident I could pull it off, but at this stage of the competition the level of talent was really high.

I strapped on this beautiful Ovation guitar and played my heart out, starting off with 'Unchained' before launching into 'Knockin''. Then it came to decision time again and they called out the names of the two acts that would go through to the final. I was just sitting there going *Please call my name out next, please call my name out next*, but they didn't. Phil Magee's band had got through and one of the other acts, and I remember feeling totally deflated. I had got so far and it had taken so long to get there. I had practised for weeks and weeks at home to get it right and then, after getting this far and not getting through, I felt like I had let everyone down, even Jono's dad. He had lent me his guitar, after all, and I felt that not only had I let myself down and let my parents down, but I had also let him down because I had failed to come up with the goods.

Everybody else thought I'd been brilliant. For the semi-finals the whole family was there and they were cheering me on, proud and delighted that I had made it so far, as I smiled and tried not to show everyone how gutted I was. My dad was hugging me but I put my head down, feeling the tears in my eyes.

I was beating myself up again, doing what I had always done, ya know, saying to myself, *You're shit, you're no good, you're wasting your time.* I had made it all the way to the semi-finals, and I should have been like, *I made it this far, I'm only 13 years of age, what an achievement,* but of course I didn't think that way. Instead I was thinking, *This is useless, what's the point?* All the same thoughts and feelings that I'd had since as far back as I could remember. This is a perfect example of what I'd later learn through therapy is called 'disregarding the positive'. And I still have to catch myself, to this day, to stop me from falling into that negative thought pattern.

And then, just before they held the raffle, the compère came back on and said they had an announcement. 'We'd like to bring back one of the performers tonight, Stephen Garrigan, as a special guest for the final.' I couldn't believe it. I was thinking, *Oh my god, that's awesome,* and my mood immediately lifted. Maybe it was a tight call for the judges and I missed going through by just a little bit so they wanted to give me something. I'm not sure why they did that but I was blown away.

So I got to go back for the final that Phil's band was competing in for the top prize. I was brought on during the intermission, and while I was still pretty nervous, I didn't have as much pressure on me because I wasn't competing and I really enjoyed it. I did 'Unchained Melody' first and then launched into 'When the Going Gets Tough' to a backing track to try and get everyone up dancing. I was singing and clapping and going 'C'mon, everyone', and it went down really well. I remember just being so happy to be there.

Phil's band ended up winning the competition. They got the big cheque and the Stephen Sheridan cup. Stephen's son Christy, who was one of the judges of the Brackenstown Talent Contest, is another well-known local trad musician and has his own studios in Swords and years later I'd use those very studios.

Before the end of the night they called out the winner of the raffle, and my dad was jumping up shouting 'Over here, over here' and punching his fist in the air. I don't know what it is about him but he was always winning the raffle, to the point that whenever there was one on we'd be like, 'Oh, there goes Des again.' I don't know what he was doing but whatever it was, it was working for him. So he went back to collect his prize, a toaster, and we were a happy bunch going home afterwards.

When we got home I went upstairs to my bedroom and quietly closed the door. I lay down on the bed and as I fell asleep I felt good, happy. That whole talent competition experience would give me a big boost, ya know? Even though I hadn't made it to the final, I knew I could do better. I had a bit of drive in me then, and I was thinking, *I've learned something new here, I'm going to keep going.*

3

AFTER THE BRACKENSTOWN TALENT CONTEST, both myself and Alan started pestering my dad to buy us a proper guitar.

The little electric guitars we had were great and all but they weren't the real deal. I remember asking Gerry what he thought was the best guitar in the world and he had said a Fender Stratocaster. And that obviously stuck in my head. To me and my brother then, and to anyone who played guitar, a Fender Stratocaster was like the Ferrari of guitars. My dad could obviously see we were both obsessed with our guitars because we were constantly playing them. And Denise was now going to Gerry for lessons as well.

We kept hounding him, and for the first while he said no, but eventually he agreed to think about it. He told me years later that he could see I had a talent and he wanted to encourage that, particularly after Brackenstown, but Stratocasters are expensive. They were probably around 1,600 pounds at the time, so it was a big commitment. He drove us up to the Sound Shop in Drogheda one Saturday and when we went in I remember him asking the guy at the counter if they could show him one of the Stratocasters. They brought one out and my dad was asking if he could pay it off every month and they were like, 'Yeah, of course.' My dad said he'd think about it.

And then we left, and I wasn't sure if he was going to go for it or not. But we all went back a week later and he told the guy behind the counter that he would take it. I was so excited that I remember thinking, *This isn't happening.* And then the guy brought it out and was putting it into its case for us to take home. This was so fantastic that it didn't seem real to me. Now, this was around November time and when we got into the car, my dad turned around and said, 'Listen, this is a Christmas present for both of you and you're not allowed to use it until then.'

Myself and Alan cradled that big black guitar case in our arms all the way home, and when we got back Dad did let us take it out and play it for a little while. But then he took it from us and kept it under his bed. There was also a set of keys that you could unlock the case with, and he hid these, so I'd sneak into his bedroom when he wasn't around and have a look for them. But I could never find them, so instead I'd drag the case out from under the bed and sit there, strumming it, pretending it was the guitar and counting down the days to Christmas.

When we finally got our hands on it, it was as beautiful as I'd imagined it would be. It was made of ash, this pale wood. I don't think they even make them like that anymore. It was just so cool. No, it was more than cool, it was amazing.

This was a professional instrument, like, we're not messing around here anymore. This was no toy that you got from Argos, this is what all our heroes would have played, greats like Rory Gallagher and Mark Knopfler, and even Scott Gorham from Thin Lizzy used one for a while. Myself and Alan were in our element and we would take turns playing it. Between the pair of us, that guitar got played all day, every day.

I was looking for any opportunity to perform again, especially now that I had this super Fender Stratocaster under my arm, and in school I got my chance. I was now in second year in 'The Bros', aged 14, and the school was putting on a big musical that was written by Mr Ó Ruis, one of the teachers. He would create this story and choose popular songs to match the various scenes. It was really clever, and when they staged their first musical the year before, I went to see it with my parents. Some of the same people who were in the Brackenstown Talent Contest were in it. It was like there was all this local talent in Swords at the time, a kinda coming of age. And I'd find over the years that I'd cross paths with some of these people who were starting out in entertainment or music or acting at the same time as me. And some of them would become good friends.

I remember being blown away by the talent of everybody involved in the musical that first year. I thought it was great. I kept thinking that I'd give anything to be up there, not acting but just singing and playing guitar, because the idea, again, of being on stage and showing people what I could do really excited me. Because it was only then, when I was up there and singing, that I could ever feel any sense of confidence.

The previous year my brother Alan, who was in fifth year at the time, had actually gone to Mr Ó Ruis and told him that he should consider me for a part because I was a really good singer and I could play guitar. Mr Ó Ruis dismissed the idea, telling Alan that I was too young, which is fair enough, but now I was a year older, so I went for an audition.

I remember most of the kids who were auditioning for

parts were much older than me. Maybe there were some other second years there too, but most were transition years or fifth years. And there were even some girls there from the Loreto secondary school, which was just down the road. I think there could have been other pupils as well, from some of the other schools in the area, like St Finian's in Swords, who would have been invited to come along and take part. I went in for the audition and I was majorly nervous, especially after seeing all the girls there. We had to go into the PE hall, where all the other hopefuls would do a dance routine or read a part from the musical that Mr Ó Ruis had prepared. And then afterwards he would put a notice up in the hall with all the names of who got what. I knew I couldn't act to save my life so I was going for one of the singing parts. Because my brother had told him the year before about me, Mr Ó Ruis kinda knew I was a singer, but he had never heard me sing before. I sang 'Knockin' on Heaven's Door' for him and one of the other teachers who was involved in the show, and he was like, 'That was super, would you like to do a part on your own?'

I was like, 'Yeah, great, I'd love to.' It was a bit daunting but I felt like this could be my time to show what I could do.

For the rest of the musical I would be in the chorus, as they call it, which is the big group of people who are in the background on the stage behind the other actors playing the lead roles. Mr Ó Ruis introduced me to the song I was to sing on my own – 'The Drugs Don't Work' by The Verve – and told me to go off and learn it.

I fell in love with that song. I practised playing it at home, over and over, until I got it perfect on the guitar and learned all the lyrics. And then I remember going in to sing and play it for the first time. We were going through the different parts of the musical during one of the early rehearsals. Mr Ó Ruis was directing all the actors and singers. They had rehearsed an acting part with somebody when he said, 'Right, now, this is where Stephen comes in.' He was waving his clipboard around, getting everyone else into place, and then he said, 'Steve's going to do 'The Drugs Don't Work', this will happen now, and then you come in,' pointing at the next person who was up after me. This would be the first time Mr Ó Ruis or anyone else would have heard me play and I was unbelievably nervous.

I walked into the centre of the room, keeping my head down the whole time. I strummed the first few notes on my brand-new Fender guitar, closed my eyes and then started singing.

I just remember everyone going majorly quiet. I couldn't hear a noise in the room apart from the guitar and the sound of my own voice. I played the last few chords and then …

silence. I opened my eyes and everyone just burst out clapping. People were coming up to me and saying, 'Holy shit, that was incredible.' Even some of the girls were going, 'My God, your voice, that was beautiful,' which was awesome for somebody like me, who was far too shy to even say hello to a girl.

Mr Ó Ruis was also clapping. 'Well done, well done.' Right up to when I started singing, nobody would have really paid any attention to me. I was just keeping quiet in the background, watching the others going through their routines and trying to blend in. But then I finally got my chance to sing, and when everyone reacted as they did, it made me relax and I felt a little bit more confident, not as shy and quiet.

After that, people started warming to me. And that felt really good. It really helped my confidence, not only on stage, but also around the others generally. Before I actually got the chance to sing and play I was almost mute in my shyness, especially with the girls from the Loreto there. But now I got a bit more attention from them. And that was awesome.

If any of the girls had tried to talk to me before then, like, if one of them had even said, 'Hey', I'd just mutter something under my breath and look at my feet. I know loads of teenage boys are like that, you know, a bit awkward around girls, but most of them probably wouldn't have had the same running commentary in their heads as I did. Like, one of the girls in the musical that year did catch my eye. She had a boyfriend at the time but it wasn't like I had the courage to go over and say hello to her anyway. It wasn't a big deal, but instead of going, *Ah, she's out of my league, so what?* I would be standing at the side on my own and I'd be beating myself up again, with the same stupid stuff running through my head, like *What's the point in even going over to talk to that girl because she's not going to like me anyway.* And worse than that, I was believing all this nonsense and taking it to heart. Once again, I'd convince myself that I was somehow lesser than I was, that I was just not good enough. It wasn't healthy and it was a bad thing to do 'cause it wasn't true. It was totally irrational, but in hindsight I can see now how it was just another example of how I used to give myself such a hard time, all the time.

I've done psychotherapy, which goes back to your childhood and what happened in your past. But I was never able to come to a conclusion or pinpoint any moment as to why I was the way I was or thought this way as a kid.

And that whole inner dialogue of negativity made me into this incredibly shy and incredibly insecure person. It would take me a long time to realise that I was doing this twenty-four seven and that it would ultimately lead to the panic attacks and anxiety, you know, all these issues that I had to deal with further down the line. I don't know where all that came from, it was just a bad habit that I had picked up somewhere but it was there all the same, and it was getting increasingly difficult to ignore.

And that held me back from meeting girls too. I would have gone to one of the local discos, like, maybe once or twice, when I was 14. You might be asked by a girl would you 'meet' her friend. And then you'd have an awkward kiss in the dark, in the middle of the disco. But I never had a proper girlfriend until years later.

After I played the guitar that day I looked forward to going to rehearsals, more than I had ever looked forward to going to school, that's for sure. Instinctively I felt drawn to perform, because, again, the only time I ever felt any real comfort or joy was when I was playing my guitar and singing. Anything I ever did involving music, or rehearsing for the musical, being on stage, or even skateboarding … that's when I was really happy and it felt like there was nothing wrong. But once I stepped off that stage I would close down again, and be back to my usual shy, timid, unsure self. It was a relief, then, if only for a few moments while I had that Fender in my hands, to play and sing. I cherished every moment I had in rehearsals. Skateboarding was put on hold while we rehearsed every Wednesday on our afternoon off from classes. I think we even had the occasional weekend rehearsal, like on a Saturday morning or whenever, in the school canteen, where we'd go through all the scenes. Then, a few weeks later, we performed the whole musical in the PE hall over three nights. They had rented a stage, and all the parents of the pupils from all the different schools came, and people from around the local area as well. They'd all bought tickets and it was a big deal. Even the local newspaper was there and they wrote a big story about it and took pictures. Mr Ó Ruis had great taste in music. And what he did was, he picked all these great songs from different eras to capture the mood of a particular scene. He had everything in there, from Tom Jones to Frank Sinatra and songs from other musicals as well, from the West End and stuff like that. I only did that one song in the middle and then for the rest of the show I was just part of the chorus in the background, but it was such an awesome experience. I loved it. I felt like I was part of something cool and, again, that gave a big boost to my confidence. I remember being blown away, watching some of the other actors who were just so good. Man, they were like … yeah, they were amazing.

I had such a great time that I wanted to do the musical again the following year but I couldn't because of the Junior Cert. My parents were like, 'Look, you have to study.' I was a bit disappointed but I understood. But the year after that, in transition year, I would go on to do it again, and I did it the following year as well.

He was great, Mr Ó Ruis, he was just so encouraging. He even offered me the lead role in the musical the following year. And later, when we got the band together in school, he was like, 'Ah, yeah, just do it, just play your music, lads, it's great and something might come of it,' whereas some of the other teachers were more practical. They'd be like, 'What are you doing? You'll never get a job doing that.' So yeah, there were some brilliant teachers in Coláiste Choilm.

I would also meet a lot of great, talented people through doing those musicals. As we grew older, we lost touch, but for a while we were all very close, and I have some great memories that I share with those people I was on stage with in those musicals. And Mr Ó Ruis? He lives in Italy now and he still comes to some of our Kodaline shows. He's a big fan.

Not long after the musical, I was at home watching Alan and his mates who were back jamming in the sitting room. Colm Maloney was using the Fender that day. He turned around to say something and the strap slipped off his shoulder.

The Fender crashed to the ground and we all jumped up.

'Colm! Oh my God, what have you done?' I picked it up and there was this massive scratch and a big dent in the back of it. Colm kept saying sorry but I remember being absolutely devastated seeing that dent there. I don't know if we even told my dad about it because I'm sure he would have been incredibly pissed off.

We still have that beautiful ash Fender Stratocaster. I gave up my share in it when I moved out but Alan still has it. Now and again, whenever I'm home, I'll pick it up and play a few chords. Then I'll turn it over and run my finger over the dent and every time I do, I think of Colm. Because not long after the day he dropped it, he was knocked down and passed away in hospital later.

Colm lived just a few doors down in River Valley View. He was a bit older than me, he was 19 when he died and I was 14. He was going to college in town, and he was on a night out when he got hit by a bus as he was running across the road. I remember walking into the sitting room one day, just a normal day, and Alan was sitting there with his head in his hands, crying. He told me what happened and that Colm was in hospital. Then he got up and ran out of the room. He had just found out from one of his other friends and he was inconsolable. Colm was his best mate. I was just this kid, and I didn't know what was going on. None of this made any sense to me and I didn't know what to do. It's all a bit of a blur now but I do remember thinking that I had just been playing football with Colm a few days before. I had looked up to him a lot. We all looked up to my brother and his friends because they were older than us, but I liked Colm in particular. He was a bit of craic. I remember him knocking in all the time and being really cool. He was such a messer. I had got very pally with Bren by then and we would be over in each other's houses all the time. And if we went to mine and Colm was there he'd rip it out of us, in a fun, playful way, slagging us and that. And now, all of a sudden, he was gone. It was very difficult for me to get my head around that.

I don't remember going to the funeral. If I did I must have blocked it out of my memory, but I do remember seeing him in the hospital. My dad brought me and my sisters in. I think Alan was already in there with his friends, Jono who was in the band with them, and another lad from down the road. Colm's mam was there by his bedside, crying. He was hooked up to life support. I remember seeing him lying there and feeling helpless, as I hoped and prayed he would wake up. We were all devastated in the car on the way home. My dad kept saying, 'See? See? Be careful on the roads, you see what can happen?'

I remember when we heard he had passed away, it must

have been not long after they had turned his life support off, I'm not sure, it's all a bit blurry. My dad was trying to console us, saying it was such a shame and that it was an accident, a horrible, horrible accident. I remember telling him, 'I don't wanna talk about it, I don't wanna talk about it,' and rushing up to my room. It had affected us all very badly and none of us really knew how to deal with it. I had never experienced anything like this before and I didn't know what to do. I picked up the Fender and ran my hand over the big dent. I traced the scratch with my finger and then I just burst out crying. I don't know if I had cried over Colm before then, but now there were tears coming fast – drop, drop, drop onto where the dent was. I remember just sitting there, sobbing. I strummed the guitar and in between heaving breaths I started singing some words, over and over again, and then I'd just lie there on my bed. I suppose by retreating into my bedroom and picking up the guitar I was trying to make some sense of it all, in my own way. I ended up writing a song, and it was about Colm. I didn't sit down and think, *Okay, I'm going to write a song about this*. It just happened.

I can't remember the name of it now, but I still remember the words. It went something like: 'Some people say, the good die young / And when they die they all become / Just like my friend who looks down on me / In the end we'll all see / Just like the leaves were falling / In this autumn of the world / I don't know, I don't know, but down we go ...'

I didn't tell anybody that I wrote that song about Colm. It was just my way of dealing with the pain of his death. At the time I felt that I had to do it, for myself, to escape. Well, no, not to escape, but to just try and understand what the hell was going on. I was so confused. Like, I could not comprehend how he could be gone, just like that. He was here the other week, playing football, and now we'd never see him again? No one close to me had ever passed away before; this was my first personal experience of death. It was rough for everyone, the whole road, and obviously for his family, and they're a lovely family too. He had a little brother, Liam, who was a year younger than me, and I can't imagine what it was like for him.

And I never really spoke about it with Alan. That sounds strange because I know it affected him in a horrible, horrible way but I think, because he was my older brother, he probably didn't want to feel vulnerable around me. That's just what I would say, you know, but for whatever reason it was like this terrible thing had happened and then it was like we had to move on and that was it.

I haven't thought about this in a long time. But it's very revealing to me now to realise that that wouldn't be the last time I'd turn to music to find solace when I was in turmoil. That song I wrote for Colm wasn't particularly good but it is the first one I ever wrote. It was very deep for a 14-year-old, but looking back on it now I can see that it came from a really sad place, and that's something that would resonate with me years later.

I understand that a song can be about nothing. It can be catchy and I'd think, *Yeah, that's an alright tune*. And when I started out in a band, that's what I did. I wrote songs that were a little bit poppy, because that's what I thought we had to do. But later, that didn't work for me anymore. Songs had to have some meaning, some purpose, to be about something. I really felt this mad need to embrace that deep, real emotion that for me makes for better, more memorable songs. And it was that deeper place of meaning I'd desperately reach out for years later, after I suffered a panic attack that would plunge me into a very dark place.

Colm's death hit everybody on the road pretty hard. As I said before, everybody knew everybody else on that road, and all the kids who grew up together when that happened remember Colm.

It even affected my schoolwork. I was in second year when

Colm died and my grades went out the window. I had my summer exams coming up but I just didn't care about studying. I was still trying to make sense of what had happened to Colm. I remember getting the results and thinking I had messed up, once again beating myself up, you know, tormenting myself with thoughts of failure and uselessness. I think my parents saw that and they understood, of course. They could see what was going on and how Colm's death had affected us all really badly, particularly Alan, who was his best mate. So they weren't too tough on me, they didn't push me too hard on the results. They just said, 'Look, it's been a weird year, it's not that important. Next year, you have your Junior Cert, so just try to focus on that.'

That summer I went to the Gaeltacht for the first time. The Gaeltacht is an area of Ireland where Irish is spoken and a lot of secondary school kids go there during the summer holidays to learn Irish. It was weird because I was still trying to process the fact that Colm was gone, taken away in this freak accident. I think I was still in some sort of shock but going to the Gaeltacht helped me. It distracted me. I think I was there for three weeks and that's a fair amount of time to be away from home for the first time, without your parents, but I had my friends there. Neale had come with me, and Bren, and I had brought a guitar as well. It was great being away with my mates. We got to stay in these different houses that we shared with lads from all over the country. Myself and Bren were in one house with a couple of other guys, from Malahide, who had also brought their guitars, while Neale was in another. We would just play, and jam together and sing. It was fun, a relief, and I really enjoyed it. You go to the Gaeltacht because you're supposed to learn Irish but I think most young lads go there to meet girls. I wasn't interested in that; for me, those three weeks were an escape and a way to take my mind off what had happened.

After the summer we returned to school, for the Junior Cert year. This was 2003. I got my head down and studied like crazy. All I did for the rest of that year was play a bit of guitar at home and take a break once a week to go skateboarding on Wednesday afternoons. There was still a big gang hanging out down there and every other week there would be new lads showing up. I got talking to one of them, a tall guy called Mark.

Neale already knew Mark. He was in 'The Bros' too, in the same year as me. I had seen him around but I didn't really know him very well, even though we lived not far from each other. Through Neale, and skateboarding, I became friends with him. It turned out I had been in the school choir with him back in Holy Family, when we were both around eight years old. We just so happened to be the only two boys in the choir and we were picked kinda randomly by one of the teachers and thrown in there with all the girls. It was like a room full of cats squalling away and I think I only went a couple of times and then managed to get out of it pretty quickly. It's funny, but neither of us really remembers that. It was only years later, when our parents got together and told us about it, that we realised we had both been there at the same time. But we wouldn't really meet again properly until we were skating, and then one day he asked me about playing guitar.

I had done Mr Ó Ruis's musical the year before and I think maybe Mark had heard I had played guitar in it. I'm not sure, because I never really went on about playing guitar while I was in school. But I suppose among the few people who played, I would have been considered quite good.

So he goes, 'You're pretty good on guitar.'

And I was like, 'Yeah, yeah, I love guitar. I have a Stratocaster.'

He told me he had just bought a guitar and was thinking of going to lessons. I told him he should go to Gerry, and he asked me would I show him a few basics in the meantime. I was like, 'Yeah, sure, I'll drop in and we can have a little jam.' So we were skating for a bit and then we all walked back home together. Neale went off to his house and myself and Mark kept going to Mark's place and went up to his room, where he took out his electric. I asked him did he know 'Johnny B. Goode' and I started showing him how to play it, but it was a bit too complicated for him. So instead I showed him how to play this simple blues riff, a really basic sequence of chords that runs through most music you've ever heard, from The Beatles' 'Get Back', and 'All Right Now' by Free, to Rory Gallagher songs. It goes all the way back to the greats, like Lead Belly and B.B. King. 'Johnny B. Goode' has this same riff but it's just played faster. So what I did was, I showed him how to play it by using two fingers to strum the same three chords. Now, if the other person plays that, you can get a scale and stick to it in the same key, and you can jam together. And anything you play in that scale will work with this particular blues riff. It's really a lot of fun when you have two people playing because one can do the rhythm part, while the other plays the lead. Then you can swap around. It's one of the easiest riffs to learn, and a great place to start learning guitar. And that was the very first time we ever played together. It was fun, and any time we jammed after that we'd spend hours doing the same thing over and over, swapping it around and taking turns to play the rhythm part and the lead.

But for the time being we were more about the skateboarding and that's how we really bonded. It would be a little while yet before we would properly start playing together. Eventually music would take over and, with it, girls and drinking, and we would kinda forget about skateboarding.

But if it wasn't for skating, I don't know if we would have ended up in a band together.

We sat our Junior Cert exams at the end of third year, in the summer of 2004. It was a high-pressure time for any 15-year-old but I did okay in them. I got a couple of As and Bs and a few Cs. I really don't remember exactly because I wasn't particularly interested in studying. I just did it because I had to, but I was happy with the results and my parents were too. As a reward they let me go back to the Gaeltacht again that summer. We had become quite pally with Mark by then so we were like, 'Oh, the Gaeltacht is amazing, you should come with us.' Bren didn't go that year, but myself, Neale and Mark headed off to Coláiste Chonnacht in Spiddal in County Galway and we brought a couple of acoustic guitars with us. I remember there was a gang of other guys in the same house as us, lads from Castleknock, who also had brought guitars, and we had great craic, all playing together and jamming. We'd be showing each other little bits of songs that we knew. I'd be like, 'Hey, can you play this?' And I'd do a bit of 'Sweet Home Alabama'. And then we'd all join in. We'd play a bit of 'Day Tripper' by The Beatles, all of us strumming that heavy guitar intro, and then 'I Feel Fine', another Beatles song. There was a lot of Beatles, but there was also 'Sweet Child O' Mine', of course, and loads of Thin Lizzy. It didn't take us long to figure out, hey, guitars are cool, there are girls here, guitars and girls are cool, so it was another win-win situation, particularly for me being so shy. Mark was less shy and more outgoing than me so we started showing off a bit.

For the three weeks we'd go to Irish classes in the morning and try to learn how to speak Irish. But in the afternoons and evenings we'd all play guitar and hang out with the other guys in the house. It was a really great time, and it was after we got back from the Gaeltacht that myself and Mark starting hanging out a good bit together. We spent the rest of that summer jamming in each other's bedrooms and practising our blues riff over and over again. I'd play the Fender and he had his electric and we'd just sit and play wherever we could and whenever we got the chance. We got quite close, and his dad invited me to go on a family holiday with them in Leitrim before we went back to school. He was like, 'Ah, it's great down there, you should come with us,' so off I went.

They had this little cottage that looked out over the lake near Lough Rynn Castle. It's a really beautiful spot and we'd actually return there years later when we were demoing songs that would make up the first Kodaline album.

I brought my guitar, and myself and Mark just jammed the whole time we were there. We would play covers, entertaining the family in the evening. One evening I played that song I had written for Colm, and Mark and his parents liked it.

Mark and myself would spend the rest of the time just messing around on the guitars. Sometimes we'd try to come up with our own riffs and ideas, but we were making it up as we went along. I'd play a few chords and then Mark would play some. We would take turns: 'Okay, you do a solo.' 'Alright, now I'll do one.' 'I want to do another one …' It was like that, just the two of us bouncing off each other and having fun. We'd literally sit there for hours jamming and playing the blues and doing solos. We'd listen to live recordings of Thin Lizzy, particularly the *Live and Dangerous* album, and Rory Gallagher and Gary Moore, and try to imitate all the great Irish guitar players. There was nothing more to it at that stage, we just played together for the pure enjoyment of it. It felt good.

But after a while, as we continued to improve, we started talking about how we could only do so much, playing together on our guitars. We both wanted to play solos but we could never stand on a stage and perform like that, just the two of us. And like I've said before, there's only so far you can go on your own, playing behind closed doors, before you have to go and put it out there somehow. We both knew this, and started talking about how good it would be to get up on stage and jam together and play solos. And then one of us said, 'You know what? We need a band, we should really get a band together.'

4

IN SEPTEMBER 2004 WE WERE GOING BACK TO Coláiste Choilm, where we had a choice when it came to transition year (TY), whether to do it or not. This was an extra year of secondary school where you didn't have regular classes and you didn't have to study for exams. Instead, it was kinda like a 'doss year', where you still went to school, but instead of going to class you had to do assignments and find work experience, out in the real world. Now, most people thought it was bizarre that anybody would want to stay back and do one more year in school than you had to. The other students in our class were like, 'Why would you do that?'. They wanted to get out of there as soon as possible and go on to college or get a job. That was the mentality. But I decided to do it. And then a couple of us kinda started trying to convince each other to do it.

I really wanted Bren to do it so we could hang out together for the year, but it wasn't as simple as that. For whatever reason, you had to go for an interview to be selected for TY in Coláiste Choilm, to see if you were suited for it or not. There were only a limited number of places in the class and I think that, in order to be picked, you had to show them why you were interested. Bren went for the interview, and I don't know what happened, maybe he didn't really want to do transition year, but he didn't get a place. And you know, I get it, fair enough. Why spend another year in school if you have the choice? But for me, I think I needed a bit more time. I didn't want to go straight into fifth year and start studying all over again. Like, for the Junior Cert I had studied really feckin' hard for the whole of that year, most of it was just study, study, study. It was draining, and I didn't enjoy it.

And I knew I was going to have to work hard in fifth year if I wanted to get into college and get onto a law course, because you had to have a serious number of points in your Leaving Cert to do that. So when it came to the option of doing transition year, which was a lot more relaxed in the sense that you could kinda do whatever you wanted, well, that appealed to me. And as it turned out, it wasn't a doss year. In fact, I think it was one of the best things I've ever done, maybe not study-wise, but it gave me a bit of time and space to really get into music. It was during transition year that I finally got to be in a band, and I would fall even more in love with music than I had ever done before. So at 16 years of age, myself, Neale and Mark went into transition year while Bren went on into fifth.

Myself and Mark had been actively trying to form a band since coming back from the Gaeltacht that summer, but it was easier said than done. We didn't really know how to go about getting a band together but I suppose the first thing we agreed on was that we needed a drummer. Mark's next-door neighbour Glen, and his older brothers Rob and Derek, had a drum kit and they all played drums. Rob was a friend of my brother Alan and had been a friend of Colm Maloney's as well. Glen was the same age as me and Mark, so we asked him did he want to join us for a few jam sessions. We went over to his house a couple of times and Glen would bash away on the drums while myself and Mark played really long solos on our guitars. Now, we had no mics, there was no singing, you wouldn't even call it a band, it was just three lads making a lot of noise. I remember the neighbours would come to the door all the time complaining about us making such a racket. They'd knock on Glen's door and they'd be like, 'Will you shut the hell up,' because you could hear us right across the estate. We did that for a few weeks, but the band wasn't really working out, so then it was just myself and Mark again, hanging out and jamming together.

This whole time in transition year, when we weren't jamming we would be skateboarding around the back of Superquinn in Swords. There was still a big group hanging around down there skating and we got talking to some of them about jamming and playing guitar and trying to start a band. One of them pointed out this guy who was skating there and said, 'You see Vinny over there? He's a class drummer.'

I knew Vinny to see because he had been there skating before, but I had never spoken to him, and I certainly didn't know he was a drummer. As it turned out, Vinny was a phenomenal drummer. And as we'd also find out, he was streets ahead, musician-wise, of myself and Mark.

A lot of skaters at the time would have been into Metallica and Slipknot, all the heavier metal stuff, and the drums in some of those songs, particularly by Slipknot, are very complicated. There's a song by Metallica called 'One' and it has this double bass drum part that is really fast. It's like, drrrm drrrm drrrm … It's super fast. And this guy we were talking to said, 'Vinny can play all of 'One' by Metallica on the drums.'

We were like, 'What?' So we went over to talk to him and asked if he would like to jam with us sometime. Now, because Vinny was such a good drummer he was already in a couple of other bands. When we asked him would he like to join us, he was like, 'Yeah, sure, but I have to rehearse with these other bands, so you'll have to fit into my schedule.' We wouldn't get together with Vinny for another few weeks, when we saw him in the Pavilions shopping centre, and that was when we agreed to start practising together.

Vinny's parents would let us make very loud music at their house, pretty much any day we wanted to. So not only did he come with the skills, the experience and a drum kit, he also came with a place where we could rehearse. Now all we needed was a bass player to complete our rhythm section, the backbone of any band.

I'd never met anyone who had played bass, so it was a bit of a mystery to me as to how to go about getting somebody who even had one. We asked around school, but we couldn't find anyone in our year who could play. Somebody mentioned this guy Conor, who was a bit older than us. He was in fifth year and we spotted him in the corridor one day and just approached him and said, 'Hey, are you Conor? You play bass, right?'

He was looking at us like, *Who are these two?* He said, 'Yeah, I play bass. Why?'

'You wanna be in a band?'

'Sure.'

It was as straightforward as that. We had our band.

Vinny's house was just across the valley from where myself and Mark lived. It was a big old Georgian house down near Main Street in Swords and it had a box room off the kitchen where he had his drum kit set up. You could actually hear the drums right across the valley. Like, they were loud. I remember walking through the valley on my way to rehearsal and you could hear the thump, thump, thump of Vinny's bass drum.

The four of us finally got together to rehearse over in Vinny's house and it was all very casual. There wasn't much to organise. Somebody would say, 'Do you want to rehearse? Let's rehearse tomorrow,' and we'd all just turn up and jam.

It was exciting, and we rehearsed, on and off, whenever we could. At the start we were a bit all over the place. It was like we were all playing our own song. We'd start off okay, with 'Johnny B. Goode', but then myself and Mark would be off doing our solos while Vinny and Conor tried to hold it all together as the main rhythm section. But it didn't matter, we were having fun, and I wanted to go over there as much as possible because I absolutely loved it. There was nothing better than playing in a room and hearing all this noise, you know, the drums and the guitars. It was way better than being at home and jamming on my own or just with Mark. And every time we went over to Vinny's, we got that little bit better.

We would play 'Johnny B. Goode' and other cover songs, which was awesome because I had always wanted to play that song with a band. We all had, like, this mutual love for that song. But I would also be writing and working on my own songs, in the background. I'd have the chords, lyrics and melody of a song that I'd bring along and the lads would play around it. Occasionally Mark would play something on the guitar, or Vinny would hit some sort of beat and that would spark something. We'd make it up as we went along, bouncing off each other, messing around and jamming while I'd sing over it with different melodies and trying different chords. It wasn't long before it all kinda started to come together.

While we were putting our band together, myself and Mark had to come up with a business idea for school, which is a big part of transition year. We were like, what's the simplest thing we can do with what we know we can do? We were both getting pretty good on guitar from all our practice, and Mark was also really benefiting from Gerry's lessons. So we decided to teach guitar to some of the younger students in school. I wasn't sure it was going to work but I do remember saying to Mark, 'Okay, look, if we only get one student or even two, that'll help pay for a couple of chicken fillet rolls for lunch.'

We put our business idea to some first and second years and, much to our surprise, we actually got a few of them to come along. We sat them down and gave them some very basic lessons. But it only lasted a very short while; they started dropping out pretty quickly. At the start we had around five, but after a week we were down to two, and then I think we only had one and that's when we decided right, this is a fail. I'd like to think that they learned something, and that we encouraged them in some way. But to be honest, we weren't the greatest teachers, because we didn't really know what we were doing. In fact, we were probably pretty terrible and I'd say it's likely that some of them never touched the guitar again.

Another big part of being in transition year was doing work experience outside of school. I actually got two placements: one was in a solicitor's firm and the other, which I was more excited about, was a week in Waltons, the famous music shop in town.

The two weeks I spent in the solicitor's office was supposed to be a great opportunity. My parents, assuming I still wanted to be a lawyer, asked my uncle, who worked for Bank of Ireland at the time and was pretty high up there, to see what he could do for me. Now, my uncle is great, he's very helpful, and a friend of a friend of his, Barry O'Neill, was a partner in a fairly well-known law firm, Eugene F. Collins. He asked Barry would he take me on for a couple of weeks and show me what it was like to be a real lawyer.

To begin with, I was just cleaning out filing cabinets and it was pretty boring. Barry gave me a few books about law, and I'd sit in his office reading them. And then he let me sit at the back of a meeting where a company had gone bust or something or they were going into liquidation. The room was full of all these debtors and creditors and they were really angry, they were effing and blinding, demanding to know where their money had gone. I just sat quietly at the back. It seemed like quite a rough situation. Barry, who was representing the company that had gone bust, was up on a stage sitting behind a table with the owners. He had to do this speech in front of all these angry people, but I didn't fully understand what was going on. It was an interesting experience but for the most part I was just an office clerk, running messages and getting coffee. I spent most of the time there on my own, but one day Barry had to go out somewhere, so he told me to go for lunch with some of the younger solicitors who were all just out of college. I remember the whole time in the café feeling that familiar unease rise up inside of me. I just sat there, silent, not knowing what to say, too unsure of myself to even open my mouth. They probably just saw me as this shy teenage kid who was in doing work experience and they didn't take much notice of me.

I was really grateful to my uncle for getting me in there, and your man Barry was great. I think my uncle said afterwards that somehow I had impressed Barry, who had told my uncle that if I worked hard and got my head down I could be there some day. I thought that was cool but I think, truthfully, I was just going along with the idea more than anything else. It was making my parents happy and, coming from a college-orientated family, I didn't want to let them down.

But what excited me the most about those two weeks was that there was another partner in that company called Carrigan, I think his first name was Michael, and his son happened to be Ben Carrigan, who was the drummer in The Thrills.

This was around the time The Thrills were starting to get really big. Their first album *So Much for the City*, released in 2003, had been massive, and a big hit in America, and they were all over the radio.

I had a part-time job at the time, working in a garage called C&T at the weekends to make some pocket money. I was filling up cars and for that whole year I was listening to this one radio station that seemed to play the same eight songs, these big hits, on a loop. There was that Natasha Bedingfield one, 'Unwritten', that I knew every word to because it was on, literally, all the time, and 'Cannonball' by Damien Rice, which is an awesome song, in fairness. But there was also that big Thrills hit 'Big Sur', which I loved. So yeah, to me they were like superstars.

When I found out I was working in an office with a man whose son was the actual Thrills drummer, I was like, *Wow!* I remember saying to Barry, 'I can't believe that his son is in The Thrills.'

'Why,' he said, 'do you like music?'

And I was like, 'Yeah, I love it. I can play guitar, and the piano. I play the drums, really badly, but I try. And I sing, and I write songs.'

And he was like, 'Okay, I did not know that. Do you want to meet Michael?'

I was too shy and reserved to talk to Michael about his son, but I was fascinated. It made it all the more real to me that it was possible to be a musician. Other bands had been successful in Ireland, of course, but here was a Dublin band, from Blackrock, who had become this massive international success, touring the world and living the dream. I was like, *I wonder how they did that?* I think it was always in the back of my mind, that curiosity about how bands made it, how they became successful. And being in an office with a guy whose son was in this huge, successful band brought it closer to me. Like, if people like The Thrills, who were from down the road and were just starting out, could do it, then that meant it was doable. That blew my mind. I think maybe that planted a little seed, you know, that maybe I could become an actual musician, after all. I never really fully believed it was possible before then, and myself and the guys never spoke about it to each other when we were rehearsing. There was never a conversation like, 'Oh we can do this, let's make a success of it.' That was never said, because we were all still very young, and our parents were like, 'You have to get a job'; that's why I was there in the lawyer's office getting work experience, after all. But it left me thinking, *What if ...* When I finished the two weeks and they asked me in school how I got on, I was just telling anyone who would listen about this man whose son was the drummer in The Thrills. But outside of that, I don't think those two weeks really did anything to convince me that I actually wanted to become a lawyer.

But my next work placement I was really looking forward to. It was in Waltons on George's Street and I loved the fact that I was going to be spending a week in this famous music shop. While I had been in the lawyer's office, Mark had been doing his work experience in Waltons, but it was the other one, across from Findlater's church, where I used to go to stage school.

I was really excited because when Mark came back after his two weeks in Waltons he was like, 'Oh man, it was so cool, they showed me how to retune guitars and change strings. I got to play all these incredible Gibsons and Fenders and anything I wanted to. They just let me mess around and it was great.'

I was like, 'Unbelievable, I can't wait.' I was thinking, *This is going to be awesome. I'm going to get to play guitars and hang out with other musicians and learn all this cool stuff.* So when I went in that first morning I was really excited. But the guy behind the counter just said, 'Here,' and he handed me a mop and pointed to a bucket and told me to go clean the kitchens.

I went into this kitchen and it looked like it hadn't been cleaned for 20 years. There were like stacks of old books and cardboard boxes, and layers and layers of dirt on the floor. I tried to scrub it off, but I'd have to go over it again and again. It was really filthy, and I spent most of that week on my hands and knees scrubbing that kitchen floor, which was pretty disheartening. I didn't even get to play any of the guitars but at least I did get to look at them. Nobody showed me how to tune a guitar or change a string or anything like that and it was Mark, actually, who ended up showing me. When I met him again we were laughing at our very different experiences at Waltons. But even though that kitchen was nasty, I was still happy to be in the shop for the week, surrounded by music. I thought it might be cool to work in a music shop one day, I just didn't want to clean any more kitchens like that one. I think I got the short end of the stick there, that's for sure.

But I did get something else out of that whole Waltons experience. There was this recorder they had there, a 10-track Zoom recorder, on display. They're expensive, but this was a used one, and it was a little bit bashed up. They said I could have it for, I think, 400 euro, which was still a hell of a lot of money. But they agreed to let me pay it off, week by week. I'd go in every weekend with the money I got from the job I had in the garage and I was actually able to buy that recorder by the time summer was rolling around at the end of transition year. With these recorders you can record your own music and listen back to it, which was a completely new experience for me. I had this SM58 mic, which is kind of a standard mic that you use on stage, and I had my Fender. I could plug them both in and play and sing and record, all at the same time. I was messing around on it, recording little bits and pieces of music, really badly at first, and then I'd put them on a tape. I remember going over to Mark and playing some songs that I had recorded and sometimes we'd work on something together. Most of the stuff I had back then would later be thrown away, but it helped me come up with some very early ideas for riffs and bits of songs that would eventually make it onto Kodaline's first album. After transition year ended I would spend most of that summer in my bedroom in the attic on my own, writing and recording demos on that 10-track.

We were back in school after the work experience, when they started auditioning for the musical later that year. I had taken part in second year and had enjoyed it so much that when it came up I really wanted to do it again. I was trying to get Mark and Neale and some of the other lads in transition year involved. I was like, 'Hey guys, we should do the musical.'

The others were looking at me. 'Why would we do the musical, that just sounds like the most uncool thing anybody could do.' They were thinking it was going to be dancing, and waving hands and smiley faces and all that stuff, but then I reminded them that the girls from Loreto would be in it. All of a sudden, they were queuing for auditions. To be honest, I think most of the guys who signed up from transition year that year only did so when they realised the girls would be in it too. This was an all-boys school, after all. I just wanted another chance to sing and play guitar, but I was thinking that if there also happened to be girls in the room and I managed to get some attention without the awkwardness of having to talk to them, then that would be a win-win for me.

Myself and Mark went to Mr Ó Ruis, who was producing the musical again that year, and asked if we could audition for a few different parts. Mr Ó Ruis seemed pretty pleased to have me back and asked if I'd like to play this song 'Superman' by an American songwriter called Five for Fighting. I had never heard it before but Mr Ó Ruis had great taste in music. As with last time, he was writing the musical and then picking all these great songs from different eras to match a certain scene, you know, to capture the mood. So I was introduced to all these other kinds of music. And that song 'Superman' is so cool. I became obsessed with it and then I was like, 'Mark, why don't you do the guitar part and I'll sing it?' Mark was well up for it so we went through the song a few times together until we got it right.

And then, at rehearsals one day, Mr Ó Ruis asked me did I want the lead role. I was blown away by the offer but there was going to be a lot of acting involved, which was completely alien to me, and I was really not sure about it. But Mr Ó Ruis convinced me to give it a shot. I think I was the only guy who could actually hold a tune, so maybe that's why he offered me the lead. But looking back on it now, I think, like, fair play to him. He gave me a chance even though he could see I was really shy. Maybe he had seen something in the first musical I had done in second year and thought that by putting me in the spotlight it would help bring me out of myself.

Either way, doing that musical definitely did help my confidence because that was something I never thought I'd be able to do. I was quite confident singing and playing guitar but now I'd have to learn all these lines off by heart and in rehearsals I forgot them many times.

In the run-up to show time I was absolutely shitting it, but when we finally went on stage for the first night I felt way more comfortable, and I actually enjoyed it. Some of my friends were there with me in the musical, and myself and Mark got to perform together on stage for the first time, which was awesome. There were full houses on all the nights and the audience seemed to like it. I can't remember what the musical in second year was called but this one was 'Primal Directive', and it was pretty out there. There was this evil guy who was taking over the world and I was like the hero in it, fighting him off. There was a love interest too and in the end the good side won out, so it was like this hero's journey. I don't think many of us actually fully understood what it was about. I mean, that's pretty bad for me to say because I had the lead role in it after all but I didn't really know what was going on either.

A few days after the musical, myself and Mark noticed that the stage was still set up in the PE hall. We had an idea. We approached Miss O'Keeffe, the music teacher and said, 'What about putting on a Battle of the Bands? You have the stage all set up, and you could sell tickets.'

She was like, 'Well, I suppose we could do that, yeah. You know, why not?'

She was all for it, which was great, and then, as word got out, all of a sudden there were bands forming left, right and centre. In the days after it was announced it seemed like every second person in school had a guitar on their back or a snare drum under their arm.

We went back to Vinny's and started rehearsing as much as we could. With the Battle of the Bands coming up we realised we needed a name, so we came up with Cold Sweat. Jaysus, even when I think of it now. Cold. Sweat. In fairness it was a Thin Lizzy song, and we were big into them, so it has something to back it up, but thank God we never went on stage as Cold Sweat. That would have been just too much cringe for me, looking back. I think that name lasted ... eh ... one week?

When me, Mark, Vinny and Conor finally took the stage for the first ever Coláiste Choilm Battle of the Bands it was as 21 Demands. We had been struggling to think of a name since we dropped Cold Sweat. The funny thing about a band's name, for me, is that it doesn't really matter. Like, it's kind of irrelevant as long as it's not really terrible, like Cold Sweat. I always thought that it's the music that makes the band. There's a lot of bands out there with terrible names who are pretty successful, and when their songs do well you don't second-guess the name. In the end it was my brother Alan, actually, who had opened up an encyclopedia and flicked through the pages. He put his finger down randomly and there it was ... 21 Demands. It's something to do with China, I think, and politics, I'm not sure. I actually have no idea, but the name stuck.

The Battle of the Bands was run over the course of one night and I think it ended up with six or seven bands in the competition. I'd say Vinny was in at least three of them, he was that good. And that would become a problem for us later on when we felt he wasn't dedicated enough to our band. We'd end up getting another drummer. He'd eventually come back to us on the condition that he left every other band he was in, which he did.

But that night we went on stage together and for the first time I got to play 'Johnny B. Goode' in front of an audience, which I had always wanted to do, from when I had first seen Michael J. Fox play it in *Back to the Future*. It was such a thrill and as exciting as I'd always imagined it would be. I closed my eyes and launched into that old familiar blues riff.

As the lads all joined in behind me, any nerves or anxiety I had before I went on just vanished and suddenly I was Michael J. Fox on the stage in *Back to the Future*. In the movie he starts playing the guitar on his head and while he's wriggling around on his back on the stage. Now, I didn't get quite as carried away as he did, but it was a lot of fun.

We also did two of our own songs that we had written specially for that gig. One of them was called 'Hold On', where I used a guitar riff that Colm Maloney had, but speeded up, and we built that song around it. The other one was called 'Why' and at the Battle of the Bands I did a terrible finger-tapping solo in the middle of it, on the guitar. It's such a cheesy, hair-metal thing to do. It was like something out of that spoof movie *Spinal Tap*. I've never done it since and will probably never do it again for the rest of my life … and I'm okay with that. Now, as a technique, it's actually quite complicated, it's something Eddie Van Halen would do, but I was no Van Halen and I did it so badly that even looking back on it now, after all these years, it still makes me cringe.

But somehow, despite my awful Van Halen impression, we were declared the winners, which came as a surprise to the four of us. Some of the other bands, who were unhappy with the result, didn't think it was such a surprise. The way they saw it, we had set up a Battle of the Bands and then we ended up winning it, so I think there were a few whispers that it was a fix. But we didn't care.

We had a lot of free time in transition year because we didn't have to study for any exams. And when we weren't jamming or skateboarding we'd hang out down in 'The Bushes', a little green area near where we lived. In River Valley there's the valley itself with a river running through it and there used to be a playground there. The pitches where I played football with River Valley Rangers are still there, and just across from that are 'The Bushes'. In the last year or two they've actually turned that whole area into this massive nature walk. Back then there used to be an old mill and we grew up hearing stories about how it was haunted, 'cause it was abandoned and a bit creepy. There was a forest there and the old mill was right in the middle of it and you could climb in and hang out, which we occasionally did. They knocked the whole thing down and now there's a big lake there, which is part of the nature walk, but at the time there were all these overgrown areas where the local teenagers would gather, to go drinking. Now,

I was fairly responsible as a teenager. I didn't really get into trouble and I was never brought home by the police, which is what happens sometimes to 16-year-olds, particularly when they start drinking and messing around. The only times the police arrived at my door was when Bren's dad, who was a sergeant in Swords, would give the two of us a lift home in the garda paddy wagon. We'd pull up outside our house and we'd get out, pretending we were handcuffed, to give the nosy neighbours on the road something to talk about. And I wasn't particularly interested in drinking anyway back then. Neither of my parents drank, although my older siblings Alan and Denise did. Me and my friends were too young to get into a pub. But then, like any teenager, you start going to house parties instead and people would be there drinking cans. I was always going to experiment at some stage, and this is where Mark came in handy. In our group Mark was easily the tallest, ya know, he's six foot six now and he wasn't far off that when we were still 16. He could easily pass for an 18-year-old, no problem, so he'd go into the local supermarket off-licence and he wouldn't be asked for ID. The very first time I went drinking I was with him, after he got a whole crate of Miller in the offy. We brought it to 'The Bushes', and we sat down and started drinking, just the two of us. I don't think we even finished the whole crate, like, I think I had maybe only four or five bottles but I was absolutely locked. I remember being really dizzy and trying to walk home, wondering, *What the hell is going on?* When I got back to my house I sneaked upstairs so nobody would see me and went straight into my bedroom and locked the door. Mark had gone home to his house too, but when he'd got in his dad had caught him and had decided to call my dad. All I remember is my dad banging on my bedroom door and he was like, 'Stephen, get up, and come downstairs right now!' I stumbled down the stairs and there was Mark's dad in the sitting room with Mark, who was trying to sit up straight on a chair. I remember thinking, *Oh no, we're fecked.* They sat us both down and gave us the big, long lecture about drinking and everything. I remember I was crying and saying, 'I'm so, so sorry, I won't ever do it again,' and trying not to get sick. I was thinking it was this big deal but it was really just a slap on the wrist. Our dads were like, 'Come on, you know you can't be going out getting drunk like this.' I learned my lesson, but it didn't put us off drinking. I'd still be hanging out every weekend at house parties, or in 'The Bushes' with all the other teenagers.

We spent a lot of time down there, and sometimes there would be girls there from the Loreto. We knew some of them who were also doing transition year, because we used to get together for social events organised by the schools. I remember we went bowling with them one time. Sometimes their transition year would come to 'The Bros' to learn woodwork, while some of us went over to them to do home economics and learn how to cook and stuff like that. They would come down to hang out in the valley and there would be a massive group that would meet at the 'Mushroom Tree', which was another gathering spot, near 'The Bushes'. We'd go down there, on a Friday or a Saturday, and there would be like 30 teenagers all hanging around, and it was great craic. And if you fancied a girl there, you'd have a chance to chat them up or whatever. There was one girl in transition year in the Loreto who would come along and hang out in the valley. I really liked her and after a few nervous attempts I got talking to her. We were just kids and I don't even know if we went out, and the whole thing, whatever it was, probably only lasted about two weeks. But at that age when you meet someone, you think, *She's the one*. Now, look, she wasn't, of course, and I find it hilarious to think how, as a teenager, I was devastated when it ended. I would go home and put on that song 'Superman' that I had done in the musical, by Five for Fighting, and I'd play it over and over again. I ended up writing this song called 'Obsession' to keep my mind off the break-up, which is seriously cringeworthy now when I think about it, because I really wasn't obsessed with her.

The lyrics were terrible but Mark had this idea for a great guitar part. We decided that a big, roaring solo in the middle of it would be awesome and after working on it a bit more with the lads, we actually came up with something quite catchy. I had this big 'oh, oh, oh', as part of the chorus and the melodies weren't too bad, even looking back on it now. It went, 'Help me out / I don't know what I should do / My head is spinning now / All because of you / I see your face everywhere I go / Oh, God help me please / you don't wanna know ...' There's another couple of lines in it, in the second verse: 'Someone told me way back when I was three / That when it hit me, I would surely see / My mind is open but my eyes are closed / So God help me please, you don't wanna know ...' I find it so funny now ... 'someone told me way back when I was three' ... like, how are you supposed to know what's going on when you're three years old? But I was only a kid. 'Obsession' wasn't the only original song I had, but it was the first one that I could stand behind because it wasn't bad, apart maybe from the lyrics, and it would encourage me to continue writing others. We would play it at some of our earliest gigs and it would become really popular among the audience, which was pretty much made up of the big group of people we were hanging out with down at 'The Bushes'. It would be one of the first songs that people learned the words to, and they would sing them back to us, which was pretty awesome. Some of them knew I had been seeing this girl and I think there was a rumour going around that I had written it about her. Now, it was written very, very loosely about that time, but it wasn't meant to be taken literally. So it made me feel really, really uncomfortable to think people were saying I was obsessed with her. I was like, 'Hang on, I'm not some creep, I'm not obsessed. We weren't even in a relationship, we were only together for two weeks, for feck's sake.' 'Obsession' would go on to do big things for us, but to that girl, in case you're reading this, just so you know, that song is not about you.

5

WINNING THE BATTLE OF THE BANDS IN TY
had given us a big boost of confidence but the problem was
that there weren't that many opportunities to play more gigs
while we were still so young, so we decided to put on our
own show. There was a local guy, from Swords, called Aidan
Cuffe and he had set up a music website called GoldenPlec.
It has gone on to do really well and it's quite a renowned
music website in Ireland today. He doesn't run it anymore.
Eventually a friend of ours, Ros Madigan, took it over with
another guy called Stephen Byrne. They run it now with a
team of writers and photographers. But at the time Aidan
was writing about different bands and promoting them and

he put on a gig in the local community centre in River Valley. We were pushing to get on the bill and Aidan gave us a spot. They set up a stage in the basketball court and sold tickets. I'm not sure if it was for charity or whatever but there were loads of other bands from around the area that played it. I remember there was one awesome band from the other side of Dublin that headlined. They were much older than us and compared to them we were way down the bill but we still got a chance to play to a bit of a crowd. Like, the hall wasn't full or anything but there were a few people there. I didn't mind, because for me, just getting the chance to stand up on a stage was good enough. And that gave us the idea to do the exact same thing and organise our own show.

We called it Fusion and we put the word out and got a few up-and-coming bands from around Swords to play at it. People paid for a ticket, it was probably like five euro or something, on a Saturday afternoon, and loads of people turned up, like friends from 'The Bros', and some of the girls from the Loreto. The other bands that were playing were from other schools so they had all their friends come along too. It was a big enough crowd and we were happy out. It was exhilarating to step out on stage in front of all those people, it was just so exciting. It was on in the same basketball court in the community centre, where I still play five-a-side football occasionally, and this time it was full. We were teenagers, in our element, showing off: 'Hey, look what we can do.' We played 'Johnny B. Goode', and 'Suspicious Minds' by Elvis, and our own 'Hold On', which, again, judging it now with the benefit of hindsight, was a pretty bad song but it did have an amazing riff. We also played 'Why', and possibly there was a bit of Thin Lizzy in there too. There's footage of that gig somewhere but I haven't watched it in years. That gig spurred us on. It was just amazing, pure escapism. I was probably terrible but I was incredibly comfortable and relaxed. This is where I belonged, on a stage, singing and playing. I was hooked. After the rush of playing in front of a crowd as part of a band, I was like, when's the next one?

We had spent the summer after transition year trying to rehearse as much as possible but what we noticed was that Vinny seemed less and less interested. We'd go over to his house but he kinda started saying, 'Aw, I can't do it today because I'm rehearsing with another band.' So eventually myself, Mark and Conor were thinking that we'd have to get someone else, you know, if he wasn't committed. It was a difficult decision but we kicked him out, and we got a friend of his, Eoin Long, who is a cool drummer, to step in. I don't think Vinny really cared, because, I suppose, he was in so many other bands, but the problem for us was that without him we didn't have anywhere to rehearse. So we rented a room in the local community centre where we had played the Fusion gig, for 10 euro an hour.

By the time I went into fifth year, in September 2005, most of the other students were knuckling down to prepare for the Leaving Cert the following year. But even though we were all supposed to be studying, I couldn't concentrate. I just didn't want to be there anymore. Transition year had been so much fun. I had just spent a year doing pretty much what I had always wanted to do. I got to be in a band for the first time, we'd won the Battle of the Bands, and I had been given the lead role in the musical. All I was really interested in now was playing music and I was happy to let it take over my life. Schoolwork would slowly go out the window and instead of studying, I was looking for any chance to get up on a stage to perform.

At rehearsals I'd be saying to the lads, 'Look, if we can't get gigs we can still do the talent shows. And if we win, we might actually get some prize money that we can use to get some professionally recorded demos done in a proper studio.' I was constantly scanning the pages of the local newspapers, looking for talent competitions that we could enter. There was a big one in St Margaret's that I had entered while I was still in third year. I had come first in the junior section, singing that song I had written about Colm. We had actually played St Margaret's the year before, while we were still in transition year, as 21 Demands, with Vinny, but we didn't get anywhere. I think back then it was still an audience-voting one and I remember when we arrived, there were a whole load of locals looking at us, going, who are these guys? Even though we were from River Valley, which is not that far away, there were a lot of St Margaret's people in the competition and it was their audience. We had nobody with us. Their whole community was there voting for their own, you know, so I think there was a bit of that going on. But it was great for us as a band in learning how to perform together, and the more we did it, the better we got. I had come a long way from when I had first got on stage in Courtown and my confidence, particularly with the lads, was getting better all the time. I'd still be nervous before going on stage and I still do get nervous, even to this day, but these were good nerves. This was the sort of adrenaline rush you need to get up and perform. We were getting good reactions too, even if we weren't winning, and that encouraged me to keep going, to keep doing this and to have some belief in my musical abilities. Now, if I had been booed those first few times, as a kid, I probably would never have got on a stage again and I wouldn't be sitting here writing this book.

Now, with Eoin on board, we entered the St Margaret's Talent Contest and this time we won. The prize was 1,000 euro, which was an absolutely massive amount of money. We decided to spend it on getting some time in a recording studio. Now, studios are very expensive, and that kind of money will only get you a day, or maybe two if you're lucky. We were never going to be able to afford that as kids so this was a great opportunity to go into a proper studio and record some songs.

One of the bands that Vinny was in had cut a demo in a studio in Swords called the Mill Studios and we thought it was awesome, so we decided to go there. It's still going, the Mill Studios, although it's in another location now and we would return there years later, as Kodaline, to record. But back then we were still pretty wide-eyed going into a studio for the first time as a band and we were amazed at all the fancy equipment. But it was a very clinical experience. I think the engineer there just saw us as a bunch of kids and we got the vibe that he wanted us in and out as soon as possible. We didn't really learn a lot from the experience but we did get to record our song 'Obsession' over the two days. And we got to go home with a CD with our own song on it. I remember putting that CD on and pressing 'play'. And, for the first time, instead of someone else's, there was our own music coming out of the speaker. That was a very special moment for me.

In school, Mr Ó Ruis was putting on his musical again, and because we had so much fun the year before, myself and Mark decided we wanted to be part of it. Mr Ó Ruis was cool with that and he asked us if we wanted to do another song together, like we had the year before. It never occurred to us to do our own song, and when we mentioned that we had this one we had written ourselves, 'Obsession', I think he was the one who suggested we just play that, which was awesome. We did an acoustic version for the musical, with Mark strumming the guitar and singing harmonies in the chorus, while I sang. I vaguely remember trying to get the audience to sing along to the 'oh, oh, oh' section and I think a few people actually did.

There was also the same set-up as the previous year, with the rented stage still there in the PE hall for a few days after the musical, so the teachers agreed to another Battle of the Bands. Myself, Mark, Eoin and Conor went on as 21 Demands and we won again, while one of the bands Vinny was in came second. I can't remember who the other judges were, but one of them was Phil Magee, who I had met at guitar lessons and who had won the Brackenstown Talent Contest. Phil had left school and was now a producer and an engineer in the Chilli Studios in Phibsborough that was owned by Brian McFadden. And the first prize was amazing, it was 1,000 euro worth of studio time in there, with Phil as the producer.

Things were really taking off for the band and Neale, our mate, who was always on the lookout for an opportunity, decided to get involved. In the run-up to that second Battle of the Bands, Neale had come up to us and said, 'Here, lads, I can get you gigs,' and he nominated himself as our manager.

He wrote up a band CV with our biogs on it and pictures of us and started going around to all the local girls' schools, handing out photocopies. He got us a gig in the Loreto, where some of the girls from the musical were in the audience. I remember he even, somehow, managed to get one of the teachers from the private girls' school, Alexandra College, in Milltown on the southside, to come to the Battle of the Bands. She watched us perform and afterwards invited us to play at their talent show, where we were the special guests. I have to hand it to Neale, his main motivation was probably just to pull girls, but in fairness, he did his job well and it's no surprise to me now that he is Kodaline's tour manager.

He also – somehow, and I've no idea how – got us a gig in the Wesley disco, the infamous 'Wes' in Donnybrook, which for us, coming from the northside, was like going to a different part of the world. This was a place well known as a pick-up disco for young teens, and even though I was in a band, getting all this attention, I was still too shy to even say hello to a girl. But I think the rest of the lads enjoyed themselves.

Somebody also sneaked a naggin of vodka in, in one of the guitar cases, so we were a bit tipsy afterwards. Neale had also organised for Vinny and his band to come along that night, to play as the support act. And I remember after that show Vinny coming up to us and asking could he get back in the band. He had seen us winning the Battle of the Bands and he knew we had won the big prize in St Margaret's, so he could see how we were taking this seriously and were trying to do something with the band. So we said, 'Right, you can, on one condition … you have to quit every single other band you're in.' He agreed, and it was after Vinny rejoined that we became a proper, serious musical act. It was a tough call letting Eoin go. He's a great guy and a good drummer, but we pointed out to him that Vinny had been in the band first, and that as much as we loved playing with him, we wanted to get Vinny back. Fair play to Eoin, he remains friends with Vinny to this day.

With Vinny back, we now had a place to rehearse again and we started searching for gigs we could play. It was very hard, though, and I think over the rest of fifth year and that whole summer we played only a couple. We may have done a few in pubs in Swords, in The Slaughtered Lamb and possibly also the Lord Mayors, which had a band night every week. Otherwise we spent most of our time in Vinny's house, rehearsing.

By the time sixth year rolled around that September I was completely immersed in music and had pretty much lost all interest in school. Sixth year was supposed to be the big year in secondary school, where you study hard for the Leaving Cert so you can get enough points to get into college. But I was completely focused on the band and trying to figure out other ways to play more gigs.

In October, we went into the studio with Phil to record some songs as part of the prize for winning the Battle of the Bands in fifth year. He was already working with some amazing people, even at that young age. At that time he was working with The Script, who hadn't done any deals yet, but he was sitting in on sessions with them. He produced some other pretty big names like Sisqó, you know the guy who did the 'Thong Song'? It's a funny story, but Phil told me years later that Sisqó was in the studio one time, doing a vocal take while Phil was in the control room, looking in. Sisqó was there with his shades on, big fur jacket, all cool like, going, 'Yo, yo, yo'. And whatever the hell he was doing, he tried to do a backflip in the studio, like in this tiny little vocal booth, and ended up completely annihilating himself and landing on the floor. So yeah, Phil, he was doing all this cool stuff and when we went in to record with him it would turn out to be a totally different experience from that first session in Swords. Unlike the engineer there, who was not really interested in us, Phil was fully hands-on. I had written and recorded rough versions of two songs, 'Paint the Town Red' and 'Sleeping on the Sun' on my 10-track at home. I had the bass, drums, guitar, and lead and backing vocals all down and the other guys liked them. Phil expanded on them and brought the production to a whole other level. He was really producing us, showing us what we had to do and guiding us. He was like, 'Okay, here's the guitar part,' and I'd play it and if it wasn't right, I'd do another take. Then I would do a vocal, and Conor would put the bass part down while Vinny was in the booth recording his drums. We were seeing, really, for the first time the dynamics of how a song was put together, but in fairness to Phil, he could make anything sound great. It was class, to be able to give our own songs the full, proper studio treatment. Almost from the very first time we had started rehearsing in Vinny's, as well as playing covers I had always been trying to create new music. I think it was just an instinct for me to try to write my own songs. Like, when I wrote that first song for Colm I think something had gone off in my head, you know? I had found a way to express myself and after that the urge to write never went away. I was interested in telling stories. 'Sleeping on the Sun' was actually about this old man I had seen walking around Swords, who always had his head down. He was this local character who everybody knew and apparently he was a really lovely man but as teenagers we were kind of afraid of him. I called the song 'Sleeping on the Sun', as if to say, he's miles away from everybody … 'Keep back out of this old man's way / He does his weekly shopping today / Is he a man on a mission / Or a man on the moon …'

There was another song I had written around these words to a lyric my brother had that really resonated with me … 'All the people that you see all around / All have their places of exile hidden deep down / You think you're strange / You think you're alone / You think you've lost the path that you've been shown / If you don't know now / You'll never know …' They were very deep for a teenager but I took them and turned them into a song I called 'No Way Out'.

Looking back on it now, some of that music was pretty cringe, and they weren't great songs. To be honest, I think they were actually pretty terrible, but I suppose we had to start somewhere.

I put 'No Way Out' and 'Obsession', as well as the two tracks from the studio session with Phil, onto a demo CD that we sent out to anybody we could think of, to get gigs and to enter competitions. There used to be this thing that RTÉ did, it was sponsored by Tayto, the RTÉ 2FM Tayto Song Contest, and I sent a copy of that CD in to enter it.

The contest was run at the time by legendary Irish radio DJ Larry Gogan, who sadly passed away in January 2020, and I got a call from him to my parents' house saying, 'I'm sorry but you're disqualified from the competition.' I was like, 'How come?' and he told me it was because we had those same songs up on our Bebo page that we had set up. By doing that we had broken one of the rules that said you had to send in original songs that had not been anywhere else.

I was like, 'Oh, well, look, I'm really sorry, we'll take them down. We have other songs we can send you.' But he told me that one of the other contestants had noticed and made a complaint so they had to drop us. I was a bit pissed off because this was a top competition with decent prizes. But at the same time our bass player, Conor, had sent a demo CD in to the TV show *You're a Star*. He never told us, he kinda took it upon himself to do that. He had sent it in, not really thinking much of it, but then he got a call back inviting us to an audition. He just came up to us one day at rehearsal and said, 'Hey, I sent in a demo and we got an audition.' We were like, 'Oh, okay, cool, if they gave us an audition, we may as well go.' We didn't think too much of it either, it was just another opportunity to put ourselves out there, so we thought we may as well go for it.

The auditions were on in the RDS in Dublin in December, and loads of acts showed up. There were hundreds of people there. Now, only a certain number of those auditioning that day would make it through to the live auditions on TV, but they didn't tell you there and then if you got through or not, so you had to wait until it aired on TV to see if you had made it. Bands and acts from all over the country were entering, and years later Jay, who is now Kodaline's bass player, told us he was in a band that had entered the same year we did but they didn't get through the audition process.

On the day we went in, it was all just bands. We were confident, because we were going to be playing 'Obsession', which we had rehearsed so many times before and had played in the musical and the few gigs we had done. That was also the song that had won the St Margaret's Talent Contest for us when we were in fifth year, and of the few originals we had at the time, 'Obsession' had become our lead song.

We arrived at the RDS and there were all these other bands there waiting to be called in. When it came to our turn we walked into a room and the judges were there, Linda Martin, Thomas Black and Brendan O'Connor, sitting behind their desks. There was another guy there as well, he could have been with Roland Ireland because the overall prize involved, I think, a record deal, a one-single record and 10,000 euro worth of Roland equipment. And to be honest, that's all I was really interested in. I mean, winning *You're a Star* and being voted the so-called best act in the country didn't really mean anything to me. I was more like, 'Wow, 10,000 euro worth of equipment would sort us out.' I was thinking we could get keyboards, amps, speakers ... They had a PA set up on this mini stage and we went on and played 'Obsession'. We got a pretty positive reaction, too. I remember the judges were enthusiastic, they were saying, 'That was great, thank you,' and then we found out afterwards that we had made it through to the live auditions.

After we got through we were told that a camera crew was going to come out and film us. It was to be a short snippet kinda thing, like you see on any TV talent show, to introduce the audience to each act. Colin, Vinny's older brother, had a friend who had a boat down in the Malahide marina and he suggested we film it there. We were like, 'D'ya know what? That would be a such a cool, random thing to do. We'd never normally get the opportunity to go hang out on a boat so let's do that.' We went down to the marina with the film crew and they filmed us as we introduced ourselves, telling the audience who we were. So it was like, 'Hi, we're 21 Demands and we're from Swords.' I vaguely remember they were shooting me sitting on the side of the boat and I was thinking, *We shouldn't have done the boat thing, it's such a cheesy idea, why did we decide to do this?* And then Conor suddenly pushed me into the water. That then went out on TV as part of our audition episode.

The live shows started in January 2007 and would go out on RTÉ every Sunday night. Each act that had got past the judges was up for the public vote so people could text in for who they wanted to go through. The four of us were getting really excited as each week went past and we made it through to the next one. This had all kinda happened out of the blue, from just sending in a demo without any big decision behind it. And now, here we were, four teenagers, still in school, and suddenly we were on national TV. In some of the early rounds we played our own songs and then there was a week when we performed the Arctic Monkeys' version of the Girls Aloud song 'Love Machine' that they played on BBC Radio 1's *Live Lounge*.

As the weeks went on they'd introduce a different theme. We had to pick a song to match the theme or they'd suggest one. I remember there was a Bowie week and we did 'Heroes'. And for the semi-final, which was a 1980s theme night, we did 'Footloose', and 'I Will Follow' by U2.

On one of the weeks the producers had said, 'Okay, whatever songs are played on the next show will be released as singles.' As it turned out, everybody else would release a cover but I said to Mark, 'No, we need a new song. This is an opportunity for us to release something original, as opposed to a cover. And I think we'd be stupid not to.' In my head I was like, *Okay, it's gotta be catchy, annoyingly catchy*, and I came up with 'Give Me a Minute'. I wrote it on my acoustic guitar at home, went over to Mark's house, sat down and played the song. There was a space for a guitar part that Mark added, we took it to the band, played around with it really quickly and had it ready for the following week's show. I don't think there is anything in that song really, it's just a throwaway tune that I wanted people to sing along to. It wasn't about anything in particular, but I suppose, if you wanted to hang it onto something, it was a very basic response to the sudden, hectic kind of schedule that we were thrown into from taking part in *You're a Star*. It was all go, go, go and it felt like we didn't have any time once we were caught up in this big TV thing. So it was like a plea to give me a moment to chill ... 'Gimme a minute, I need a minute, Gimme a minute / Have you got any time at all / Am I running out of time ...' Looking back on it now, I don't rate that song at all, it's very lightweight, but I do remember when we played it the first time on the show they had a guest on, Tony Hatch is his name, who had written the theme tune for the TV show *Neighbours*. I remember being incredibly intimidated, I think we all were, because he was this big, well-known songwriter and I felt we were just chancing our arm with this song we had pretty much made up on the spot. So we played it, and he actually said something like, 'Great lyrics, great melody, but I would have gone somewhere else in the middle eight.' Like, it was fairly positive. He didn't rip us apart, which was a relief because he was known to be very cutthroat. I remember my parents saying that he was involved in some other talent show years before in the UK and he was known as the guy who would tear acts to pieces. Like, he wouldn't be afraid to say, 'You're absolutely awful, what are you doing here, get off the stage,' but he was kind to us, and that's a memory that stands out. And then, when the song was released, I remember being told that we had become the first Irish band to go to number 1 through downloads alone, and that was unbelievable. From playing random pubs here and there to having the most downloaded song in the country … it was amazing. It was zero to 100 and we were like, 'Wow, this is mad, holy shit.'

Now I genuinely believe that if it wasn't for the show, that song wouldn't have gone anywhere because we were just riding on the wave of being on the TV every other week, but it was incredible when it happened, and it blew our minds.

Every week we'd do the show in The Helix, a venue on Dublin's northside, and then afterwards head over to Wright's café in Swords to watch the results. Colin knew the manager there at the time, Alan Clancy, who let us gather there every Sunday, and that became our unofficial band hangout during *You're a Star*. All our families and friends would be there, watching on the big screen, cheering us on and celebrating each time we got through. We'd play live in The Helix that evening and then there would be like a gap of a couple of hours before the results show came on so we'd rush over to Wright's, all nervous because we had no idea if we had made it through or not.

When *You're a Star* kicked off, Colin kind of stepped in as unofficial manager. Neale, who was fairly studious, had decided, because it was sixth year, to focus on studying, so Colin started looking after the band. He got cards printed up with '21 Demands' written on them and the numbers that people could text to vote for us. He handed them out everywhere, and he also arranged for us to go into the local schools to sign autographs. Colin was brilliant at that stuff, he'd drive around in his jeep with big stickers on the side saying, 'Vote for 21 Demands'. Vinny's older sister, I think, also had a jeep, and between all our families and friends there were a lot of people driving around Swords with big 'Vote for 21 Demands' stickers plastered all over their cars. It really took off, like, you know, our whole community rallied around. Everyone got behind us and there were banners out over River Valley and posters up on walls in 'The Bros'. I remember going into nightclubs in town with Neale and I think Mark was with us too, handing out flyers. And people were starting to recognise us, the odd person in a local shop would say, 'Hey, 21 Demands!' or they'd shout across the street.

There was a lot of excitement building up and I remember going into the final that was held over two nights and thinking, *We can do this*. We chose to do 'In the Morning' by Razorlight, who were a huge band at the time. We figured it was a good, current song and it felt right. We also performed a song called 'Courtesan' that we had already played on the first night. I had written this song about a girl I had met at the 'Mushroom Tree' one night. If you remember, I had first spotted her at the musical all the way back when I was in second year. Anyway, I had started kinda talking to her and we were texting each other for a while. But then one night, I was coming back from the 'Mushroom Tree' when I got a text from her saying that she was getting back with her ex-boyfriend so I was a little bit pissed off. There's a bit of anger in that song, kinda like, 'I don't need you anymore' sorta thing. It was a song with some weird lyrics. I think I was drunk as well, coming back late that night from the 'Mushroom Tree' when I got the text. I sat down on the couch, picked up the guitar and started singing: 'It was late / I was tired / I should have known but I was wired ...' I was sad, I suppose, and a little bit bitter. It's kinda stupid. And I didn't even really know what the word 'courtesan' meant. I just thought it sounded cool.

So the final went to the public vote, on live TV, and David O'Connor, a solo artist, beat us. I remember being pretty devastated when we didn't win. I think we all were, and there were loads of people around us saying, 'Oh, you were robbed.' But what happened really quickly was that because the TV show had put our name out there, all these offers of gigs and requests for appearances and stuff like that suddenly started coming in. We had a band email set up at the time and we were getting messages from pubs and venues all around the country, asking if we were available. Right up until that moment we had been banging on doors trying to get any gig we could and now people were calling *us*.

Even though we didn't win, that whole *You're a Star* experience was awesome and now we were getting all these gigs on the back of it. Wright's café had us play every other Sunday too and all our friends and family would come down to watch us. I met that girl again on one of those nights at Wright's, the one I'd written 'Courtesan' about. But now she was single again and we kinda hit it off. We started going out with each other and she became my first serious girlfriend. The whole thing was great, you know, it brought all our families together for the first time, and Vinny's parents and my parents and Mark's and Conor's all got to know each other. We'd also gather in Vinny's house and hang out and talk about the band and *You're a Star* and how we might get a record deal out of it. It was a very happy, exciting time.

With all these gigs coming in, Colin, who had been looking after the band during *You're a Star*, took charge. It just happened naturally. He knew a lot of people and, yeah, he was definitely the right guy for the job. It was like, 'Great, Colin can look after all the bookings and arrangements and we'll just focus on playing.'

And because we were getting paid for them too, we could rent a PA system and play anywhere we wanted. Colin rented a van and we'd put the PA system in the back, climb in on top of it and head off down the country. There were no seats in this van, you know, it was just the basics and I remember lying on the speakers with all the gear in the back. It was really uncomfortable but so much fun. We were going all across the country, to play in a different county every other day. I couldn't believe it, I was like, 'Holy, shit, I'm in a van, going to a gig somewhere down the country to play music, and we're getting paid for it.' Now, we were coming out with feck all. I think the odd gig was paying us like, maybe, 1,200 quid, which was a lot of money. But then, when you think about the cost of renting the PA system and the van and then splitting what was left between the four of us who were in the band, there wasn't much left. And then there was Colin to take care of, so we were probably getting like 100 quid each into our hands. But I didn't care. Getting into a van to go gigging down the country, to Galway or Limerick or wherever, for me, we may as well have been touring America.

We'd rock up to some place where we had been booked to play, most of them would have been small local pubs, and there would be a poster in the window, and flyers handed out: 'Tonight, 21 Demands! As seen on *You're a Star*'. We were getting decent crowds too, mostly young people, and they would be up singing and dancing. We would play for a full two and a half hours each night. We'd have to cram the set full of covers to fill out the time. We'd play old reliables like 'Johnny B. Goode' and some of our own songs that we would have performed on the show, as well as a few others. It was a great way of honing our sound but I think at that stage we were already pretty tight as a band. Like, during *You're a Star*, we had the show every Sunday but we would be rehearsing twice or three times that week, going over and over again any particular song that we would be playing the following Sunday. So we were pretty good.

Some of the gigs were odd, though, and as the weeks went by they got more bizarre. I remember one we played in a basketball court in a community centre in Lacken in County Mayo; it was a daytime gig, for the local scouts, I think. I just recall getting out of the van, it was still early in the afternoon, and setting up the gear, but there was absolutely nobody there. We were looking at each other, wondering what to do, when suddenly two massive coaches pulled up and hundreds of kids jumped out and ran screaming into the hall. It was some kind of kids' disco and we were on as the main act afterwards but the kids were going mental, running around and jumping up and down.

I was caught up in this whole thing that had just taken off and it was so exciting. We had gone from playing local talent competitions to this massive national TV show and now we were gigging all over the country. It was mad. I remember, right in the middle of the Leaving Cert, me and Mark sat an exam one morning, and as the lads travelled down in a van, we flew to Cork to do a gig straight after. And then we flew home again that night because we had another exam the very next day.

That gig, actually, was one of the stranger ones we did. It was for a farming festival in west Cork, or something like that. They had a limo pick us up from the airport to drive us to the festival. We got off the plane and walked out, feeling a little bit cringe about getting picked up at the airport by a limo to go to a gig. It was such a cliché, but then this rusted, beaten-up, battered beast of a thing pulled up. It was like something from the 1980s, you know, and it was so old and smelled so bad that we didn't even want to get in. We were like, 'What the hell is going on?' We just found it all absolutely hilarious and laughed all the way to the gig in the back seat while the driver stared at us in the rear-view mirror. It brought us to this farming festival thing and I remember there were all these sheep walking around. I think it was one of those competitions where they pick a winner, I don't know, the most beautiful sheep or whatever. There was something very *Father Ted* about the whole thing. We went into this office with Colin to see the guy who was running the festival. Colin was trying to talk to him about the fee and how much we'd get paid and stuff. I don't know why I remember this, but the guy was sitting at his desk in this tiny little cabin-type thing, like a Portakabin, and we were all kind of squashed in together. There was a sign on the wall that said 'Sheep!' for no apparent reason. Just one word … 'Sheep!' The guy was counting out all these grubby 50-euro notes and putting them on the table while we stood there awkwardly. Conor was nudging me, pointing to the sign, while I tried not to burst out laughing. And afterwards he was like, 'Did you see that sign?'

We were looking at each other going, 'Where the hell are we?'

The stage was on the back of this truck in the middle of a field so we climbed up and set up the PA and the drums and all the equipment. It was another early-afternoon gig and we must have played for two, two and a half hours. Everyone was sitting out on the grass and there were probably about 100 people spread out, but most of them were chatting to themselves and not really listening to us. But then this guy stood up and he started dancing so I kinda played off him because we weren't getting a whole lot of reaction from the rest of the crowd. But the crowd started to enjoy him and his antics more than they were us, and he eventually got people standing up, dancing and joining in. Afterwards, we found out his name was Chicken George. I don't know why they called him Chicken George. He was obviously an eccentric character, that one person in the town who everyone knew and seemed to love, and fair play to Chicken George, he got the crowd going.

Yeah, that was very bizarre. I think of all the gigs we did that was probably the weirdest one. No, wait! There was another one. I think it was in the Set Theatre in Kilkenny, where we were the special guests at some sort of song contest. Colin couldn't bring us to this one so his older brother Anto brought us instead. And it was particularly strange. It was like this song contest where everybody had written their own song. It was a 'song of peace' competition, that's what it was, and it was in this small little theatre. We were paid, I think, 1,000 euro to be the special guests. All the songs being performed in the contest were quite calm and spiritual. Most of the audience there were way older than us, like they were in their forties and fifties, sixties possibly, and some maybe even in their seventies. I remember one of the acts, they were all wearing white suits, with full make-up and long hair, and they were singing all these kinda Christian songs. It was like a really, really, really, dodgy Eurovision and I have no idea why we were booked to be special guests. We went on during the interval and loads of people left, there was hardly anybody in the crowd. But this old couple, now these must have been in their seventies, were still sitting there and they had been enjoying the peaceful, meditative vibe. And then we came on and went into 'Give Me a Minute' or, I don't know, 'Johnny B. Goode', something that was really fast, and loud, and the old guy just put his hands over his ears and sat there glaring at us. There were only about 20 people left in the audience at this stage but we just kept playing, as if it was any other gig.

You know, there is one other amazing thing that happened off the back of *You're a Star* and I want to mention it now because it would turn out to be pivotal in the formation of Kodaline. We got a call from Ronan Keating. He grew up in Highfields, which is just like two roads down from my parents' house, but he lived in Malahide at the time, in Abington. Conor and his uncle both worked in Dublin airport, and Conor's uncle gave Ronan a copy of our CD when he saw him going through the VIP lounge. Ronan later invited us over to his house, and said, 'I've been watching the show with my kids and they're big fans,' and we actually signed autographs for them. He offered us the use of his own private studio, which was an amazing offer because we were smashed broke then and studios are expensive. He just made this great gesture, and then he was like, 'Look, if you ever wanna use the studio, I have it there, anytime.'

And we were like, 'Eh, yeah, thanks!' I think at that time it gave us a lot of encouragement as well. And for me, personally,

I was like, *Wow, if he's willing to help us, he obviously sees something in us.*

Now, he didn't have to do that, but he did. There were all these people who would help us along the way and he was one of them. And, as it turns out, what he did for us would prove to be invaluable.

The finals of *You're a Star* were held in The Helix on 18 March 2007, just three months before the Leaving Cert exams started. I probably could have managed to sit them, if I had worked hard and tried to focus, but that was never going to happen because of all these gigs that we had coming in.

For me and Mark, sixth year in school had gone completely out the window. Conor had already finished school, he was a first-year apprentice electrician in the airport with the Dublin Airport Authority, and Vinny was a year below us, in fifth year, so it didn't really affect them much. But for me, to be honest, I had already lost all interest in school, even before *You're a Star* kicked off. Up to the Junior Cert I had been very studious in class and had done well enough to keep up. But during transition year music had become my life and my education had slowly slipped away. And by the time *You're a*

Star happened, I was like, 'Okay, I'm going to fully commit to this instead.'

In my head, I had given up on the Leaving Cert, long before the exams started. I accepted that there was no way I could fully dedicate myself to studying for it, and so there was no way I was going to get the points I needed. And because I knew I wasn't going to do well in the exams, I just kind of stopped going into school as well. Every time we made it to another week on *You're a Star*, the less I went into school. After the show went out on the Sunday I'd be very reluctant to go in on the Monday. I might show up on a Tuesday instead. But whenever I did show up, people would be like, 'What are you doing here? I thought you'd dropped out.'

Also, because I was on TV every week, people were starting to recognise me, and possibly that was another reason why I didn't want to go to school. Like, I remember feeling more and more uncomfortable walking through the halls in 'The Bros'. We had become something like minor celebrities, and people in school would say, 'Hey, Steve, how's it going? Good luck next week.' Part of me liked it, and made me think, *This is good, we're getting more attention, maybe the band is doing something, going somewhere.* It convinced me that the show was a good opportunity for us but there was also a part of it that made me feel so incredibly uncomfortable. I had never experienced anything like this, you know? Like, people who would never have even looked at me before, all of a sudden they were my best friend. The fact that I was a really shy person anyway didn't help when all that recognition thing, even on a small level, started to happen. It just weirded me out. But I suppose it did help my confidence. It felt like I had a purpose, and that made me, in a way, happier. Not that I still didn't have my insecurities, and my shyness, but I did feel good about the whole thing.

There was probably a point or two where I was called into the head teacher's office to explain why I was hardly ever there but I just made excuses and assured them I'd do better.

I don't think my parents realised how much school I was missing. I was getting away with it because both of them worked. Most days, by the time I had to leave for school they'd have already left the house. And then I'd pretty much stay at home, playing my guitar. There was the odd day that I'd pretend to go to school and then, when my parents were gone, I'd sneak back in. Sometimes, if they were at home for whatever reason, I'd leave and come back early, making up an excuse that I had a half day.

In the back of my mind I was like, *Okay, we have a chance here. We could make it.* I don't know about the other lads, but I was thinking, *Something big, something amazing could happen … we could possibly make a career out of this.* Part of me was like, *Okay, I'll see what happens over the summer. We might get a record deal out of this or we might get something that could push this forward. And if it doesn't, and if the worst comes to the worst, I'll just go back and repeat my Leaving Cert and try to get into college the following year.*

I didn't tell anybody in school, any of the teachers, or my parents about my plan. So I was pretending the whole time, trying to give the impression that I was working hard and making an effort, but I wasn't at all. I hated being in school. All I wanted to do was be in a band and play music. If I was in a van, on the road to a gig with the guys, I was happy. Everything else just bored the hell out of me.

After *You're a Star* kicked off I barely even opened a book between then and the exams in June. I don't think I even turned up for some of the exams because I had just accepted that, not having done any work, there was no point.

When the results came out I hid them and never even showed them to my parents because I knew I would get a bollicking. On the day I was supposed to go in and collect them, I didn't even bother, and in the days that followed I remember waiting anxiously for them to arrive in the post. And then, when they did drop through the letterbox one morning I quickly picked up the envelope and rushed to my room. I stood there looking at it. I wasn't even going to open it, but eventually I did. It was bad. I had failed a couple of subjects, and even with a quick glace I could tell I only got about 240 points or something like that. And to get into law, for example, you would need a lot more than that. Compared to my Junior Cert, it was a disaster, just as I had expected, so I scrunched up the paper in my fist and threw it behind a desk in my bedroom. Years later I actually found it, still lying there in a ball, and eventually I threw it in a bin. My parents asked me about the results on multiple occasions but I always found a way to deflect their questions. We'd also later agree that I would repeat the Leaving anyway, so it was eventually dropped.

For the rest of that summer I remember the four of us hoping that we could get some sort of record deal on the back of *You're a Star* and so we continued to record our own songs with Phil. At this stage he had his own little portable set-up and he would come over to Wright's, where they had given us this spare office to rehearse in. We had actually moved from Vinny's to rehearse in there and we demoed maybe five or six songs with Phil in that room. We were recording pop songs in the vein of 'Give Me a Minute', throwaway poppy guitar songs, but I don't think they were any good.

At some point over that summer, a few months after the

show aired, we got a call from the same record label that had offered the prize of a record deal for the winners of *You're a Star*. They offered us a deal, but it was only a one-single deal for 'Give Me a Minute'. I was surprised that we were even offered a single deal because the song had already been released and had gone to number 1. We had actually been working on re-recording it with Phil because we thought the version that had been released was pretty rough. We didn't know anything about record deals and because we had been recording with Phil, we asked him what we should do.

He had said at one point that if we were offered a deal like that, to turn it down. He was pointing out that it would just be banking off the exposure we got from *You're a Star*. He was saying, effectively, 'You'll release the song and that will be it.' He told us that what we needed was a development deal. This is where a company invests in a band. They pay for studio time and give the artists time to grow, to find their feet as songwriters and evolve their sound, before they even start to work on an album. That's what we wanted, but they were never going to do that for us. So, yeah, we took Phil's advice and turned down that deal and we never heard from them again. Phil was right, by the way. A single-record deal wouldn't have got us anywhere and we would have been wasting our time. But development deals are hard to come by and ultimately, we would end up developing ourselves. And then, after that, it was pretty much coming up to the end of summer and I had to make a decision: repeat my Leaving Cert or try to do things with the band. But there wasn't really anything happening – as quick as our 15 minutes of fame had arrived, they had gone even quicker.

You're a Star was an amazing experience, it was great, and it gave us a taste of how things could have been, if they had worked out. But I think at the time we were so young that we may have got caught up a little bit in thinking that this could work and we might get a career out of it. And you know, there is an element of truth there, like, maybe we could have made something of ourselves from *You're a Star*. It was a great platform and I mean we did get a lot of gigs off the back of the show. But I also thought there was a chance we could walk away with a proper record deal and a real shot at making it as a band. But we were naïve too, like, we didn't even have that many songs of our own to begin with.

And by now the attention that we had got from the show was starting to fade away and the gigs were drying up. We still got a few offers but they were few and far between and then, over the course of the summer, they just kinda stopped coming in. The band's email inbox was empty. We had continued to play every other Sunday afternoon in Wright's, which had led to them letting us rehearse there. We spent most of that summer recording in there and using it as a rehearsal space and then we were told one day that we couldn't use it anymore. I think, for me, that was the final realisation that we had gone from minor TV stars to being left high and dry. It was during that summer, while all this was going on, that me and my dad sat down and had a talk. He said, 'Look, you're trying with the music, but you have to have a fallback plan.' He was saying to me that getting on *You're a Star* and playing all these gigs had been great and all, but what if it didn't work out? Of course, a big part of me was like, 'I really want this to work,' but at the same time, deep down, I think I already knew there was no way it was going to happen. I said to my dad that I had already thought about repeating my Leaving Cert so we agreed on a plan so I could get into college. We spoke more about it and I knew he was right, but I was gutted. There was some talk about repeating in Coláiste Choilm but I was fairly adamant about not going back to 'The Bros'. Going back there would have made things a hell of a lot worse for me. Having to repeat the Leaving Cert at all was depressing enough, especially after our brief flash of success. I had really wanted it to work out but that didn't happen. And now, having to go back and repeat the Leaving Cert was proof to me that I had failed with the band and that it was all over. That was something

I had just decided in my head was true, which is, of course, just more of the negative thinking that I subjected myself to. I know now, looking back on it, that that was completely wrong, but after the year we'd just had, with *You're a Star*, and the band taking off and all the attention and the possibility of making something with music within our grasp, it felt like I was going straight back to square one. And as bad as all that was, I'd also be going back to the same school where people knew me. I didn't admit this to my parents but I thought that by going to a place where I didn't know anybody, I would be better off because at least that way I wouldn't have to explain what happened and face the shame of failure and all the questions, like 'Why are you repeating? Are you not doing music anymore? What happened to the band?' This is what I thought would happen if I went back to 'The Bros', and I felt like it would be a horrible experience to put myself through.

My dad was like, 'Okay, look, if you're really going to get your head down and work ... if you want to get into law, I'm willing to send you to the Institute in town, but you have to commit.' It was an amazing offer and very generous, because it's like five or six grand a year or something to go there. In my mind I accepted that this was the way it was going to have to be. But it was that year, in the Institute, when everything started to really fall apart.

6

I THINK THAT *YOU'RE A STAR* AND EVERYTHING about the show, playing live on TV, performing our own songs and covers, going back to Wright's, where all our family and friends were ... all of that was amazing. But anything else outside of that made me feel very self-conscious and uneasy. Like, I remember walking through town one day shortly after the show had aired and some woman shouted across the road, 'Hey, 21 Demands, I love you.' There were a few little moments like that, where people would recognise me, and it made me really uncomfortable, but I was even more uncomfortable when our 15 minutes was up and I found myself back in school.

By the time I was going back to repeat my Leaving Cert in September we were only playing the odd gig here and there, and in terms of offers and invites, yeah, they had come quickly but then they were gone even quicker. I went from being on TV every week to sitting on a bus, going back to school. In what, a matter of months? It was a very sharp let-down and my thinking then was that it was all over. It wasn't, of course, we still had a long away to go as a band, but as far as I could see, as I walked through the doors of the Institute on Leeson Street that very first morning, the dream of making it in music was fading away into the distance.

There was pressure on me now. I knew my family had spent a lot of money so that I could go to the Institute. It was a privilege but it is expensive. and it is an incredibly good private school, you know, in terms of, their having a track record. Like, if you need to get a certain number of points, and you work hard, they will get you that number of points.

But I remember almost from day one, going in there and, like, walking through the halls and just feeling really, really nervous. I think it was then that the underlying anxiety I had always felt, that was always there, just under the surface, started rising up and it became an almost constant presence. I had always been incredibly unsure of myself, and now, I think, I was also a little bit broken and deflated. I felt there was no longer any hope with the band and that was really eating me up. It was irrational, I can see that now, 'all or nothing' thinking. And little did I know that I would ultimately end up playing music and becoming a professional musician, doing what I love. But at that time, the frame of mind I was stuck in convinced me of the opposite. After *You're a Star* I had convinced myself that we really did have a chance of going somewhere with the band, that maybe I could have a career as a musician, just like that man's son who was the drummer in The Thrills. But as the weeks passed it felt like the idea of the band being in any way an option was drifting further and further away. The rest of the lads had either already done their Leaving Cert and were going on to college, or they had part-time jobs or whatever, so we were all moving on, each in our own way. Like, Vinny got a job, I think he was in an apprenticeship with his brother fixing cameras or something like that, and Mark was working in a call centre. Conor was still working in the airport as an electrician so not that much had changed for him. At the same time, the band was still there and we would even have the odd rehearsal, but not many. And in the meantime, here I was, back in school, knowing almost straight away that I didn't really want to be there, but feeling trapped, because I had to do it after my dad forked out all that money.

Because I had given up on the Leaving Cert the first time around, now I was putting extra pressure on myself. The way I had always been beating myself up, well, that pressure was ten times worse now, because now I had all these 'what ifs' racing through my mind: *What if I fail? What if I don't get the points? What if I have to repeat again? What if I don't get into college? What if I never get a job?* It was like this constant worrying and stressing. In hindsight – and, yes, it is a wonderful thing – I shouldn't have been so hard on myself. I was only a kid, but – and this is so important to know this – I didn't talk to anybody about anything then. So if I was having a bad day or feeling particularly nervous or anxious, and anybody asked me how was school, I would just say it was great, you know, even after I had just spent the whole day walking through the halls on my own with my head down.

I didn't know anyone there so I went back to being that kid I had been in school, keeping myself to myself. But now I was fading into the background more than I had ever done in 'The Bros', or in primary school. If I caught eyes with somebody I'd quickly look away.

All the fears I had about going back to 'The Bros' and having to deal with that came up in the Institute. I had all these nagging thoughts … *What if they recognise me? What if on the off-chance they had seen the show, well, now they could see*

I was back repeating my Leaving Cert. It was bonkers, I know, but that's what was going through my head, constantly. Like, *Feck, I'm going to have to talk to them. And then they're going to ask me what I was doing, why was I back repeating my Leaving Cert and what had happened with the band and was I not doing music anymore.* On and on and on.

If somebody would ever, on the rare occasion, ask me about *You're a Star*, particularly in the Institute, I'd try to change the subject as quickly as possible and walk away. I was there to study, to repeat my Leaving Cert, and that was all, and I didn't want people bringing up anything to do with *You're a Star*. I had come to the conclusion that I was a failure because the band hadn't worked out. And because I had convinced myself that I was a failure, I was afraid other people would think that too, even though, in reality, 99 per cent of them didn't even bat an eyelid and wouldn't even know who I was. But I was embarrassed and I just kinda wanted it all to go away, almost to the point where I wished I had never been on that show.

That was the thinking that I had back then, which is completely irrational, I know now, but it sent me spiralling down into a place of real doubt and shame. I became further and further distanced from the other students around me, and it wasn't long before I started skipping the odd class, once I felt I could get away with it. There's a thing in the Institute where the teachers give you these notes for each class. And the notes are everything, you don't even necessarily have to go to the class if you have them. So I'd take the notes that were handed out and then go and sit on my own in a café and try to study them. But I would spend the whole time beating myself up, blaming myself and thinking that my whole music career was completely over and we'd never have another chance at making it as a band. That's the way I was thinking … black or white … all or nothing. But I don't think I realised how much it affected me. I think I was ignoring the fact that I was devastated that, at least in my head, the band was over and there was now no possibility that I could pursue music as a career. But I knew I had to do something. So I just got on with it. I was able to focus in class, and study, even though I didn't really want to be there. I was only there to please my parents really but I wasn't happy and I'd slowly fall further and further into a deep hole.

I don't know, but I think that after the fallout from *You're a Star* had faded, it really did do a number on me, and my confidence and my belief in music had been seriously rattled. For me, the dream of ever having a career in music or even getting a chance to do anything music-related ever again, from writing songs to performing, had disappeared.

Music had been, up to that point, one of the few things

Alan, Denise, Fiona and me.

At Christmas 1999, I performed in the *Sleeping Beauty* panto in St Anthony's Theatre on Merchant's Quay as part of a Boyzone tribute act called Boyzonly. I played Ronan Keating.

I was 13 in this photo and taking part in the Brackenstown Talent Contest. I did a cover of 'Unchained Melody' – it was the first time I sang and played guitar during a performance.

As 21 Demands we made it through to the final of *You're a Star* in 2007. We would eventually change our name to Kodaline.

This is one of our first ever gigs, at Swords Community Centre in 2003. One of the many times I played the Fender Stratocaster my dad bought for me and my brother Alan to share.

Some video stills from a gig 21 Demands did in 2006 – with Eoin Long on the drums – at Loreto Secondary School, the girls' school down the road from 'The Bros'.

Playing The Academy, Dublin in 2012 shortly after the release of the *Kodaline* EP.

A moment of peace after a run in Howth, County Dublin. Taking up running is one of the best things I've ever done – it really helped me get back on my feet after my first panic attack and remains an important part of my self-care.

My girlfriend Diana has been with me through some of my lowest moments and has always been there for me.

Songwriting at home. Writing music and lyrics is something I've enjoyed for a long time, but it also became – and continues to be – a really important emotional outlet for me. It always means so much to hear a crowd singing the words of our songs along with us.

Playing The Sugar Club in Dublin, 2012. We sang 'All I Want' and the crowd erupted. It was one of those moments when we all looked at each other and I thought, *This is actually happening*.

Performing three gigs at the Olympia, Dublin, in November 2013 was incredible. The Olympia Theatre is such an institution in Ireland. It was after one of these gigs that I met my girlfriend, Diana.

Returning to where it all first started! In March 2013, we visited Coláiste Choilm CBS in Swords, which was where Mark, Vinny and I met and began playing together.

I painted this hand on the wall while I was a student at 'The Bros'. It was amazing to go back with Mark and Vinny to revisit all the old memories.

The O2, Dublin, March 2014.

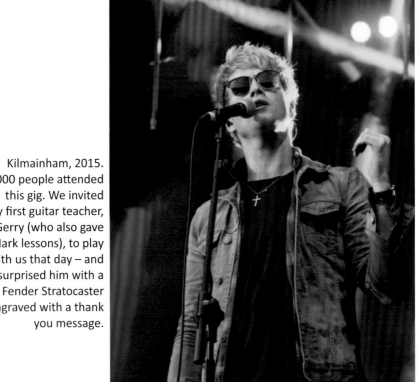

Kilmainham, 2015. 15,000 people attended this gig. We invited my first guitar teacher, Gerry (who also gave Mark lessons), to play with us that day – and surprised him with a Fender Stratocaster engraved with a thank you message.

CP5

Vinny (holding the microphone), Jason and Mark explain to the audience at the Bikini in Barcelona that I had to be taken to hospital by ambulance and that the show was cancelled, 4 March 2016.

We headlined two shows in St Anne's Park, Dublin in 2019. Both nights we played 'Angel' from the *Politics of Living* album – a song we wrote in memory of Ciara Lawlor.

Writing and recording *One Day at a Time*, our fourth album, at our studio in Dublin (which we refer to as 'Kodaline HQ') in spring 2020.

Backstage during Kodaline's UK tour in November 2019. Life on the road has its ups and downs but, at the end of the day, myself, Vinny, Jason and Mark are like brothers and I feel incredibly lucky to have them.

I had that I could actually escape into, to make myself feel better. It was something I thought I was good at, but it had put me in this very weird, uncomfortable situation. Now, the one thing in my life that had offered some solace and some relief from this constant unease had led me down a very weird path. I had always been happy when playing music, always comfortable and calm when singing and playing guitar ... but I wasn't so happy with what came after that first sudden flash of fame. It had never occurred to me what might come with any bit of success, it was all just about playing music and enjoying it. That was it.

On a very small scale we got to feel that little bit of attention and recognition on the back of *You're a Star*, particularly when, during the show, as I mentioned earlier, we'd go round to different schools and ask people to vote for us and stuff like that. The kids would be all like screaming and asking for autographs, and while it was bizarre for all of us, I think the fact that we were actually just four normal lads who supported each other meant that we saw the funny side of it. But suddenly it had all ended and we were off doing our own thing again. It was like real life had interrupted the dream. Now that I think about it, we never really discussed the effect that being on *You're a Star* and then finding ourselves going back pretty much to our day jobs had on any of us. I never spoke to the lads about it; we just focused on what each of us was doing and the band took a back seat. And pretty much then, for the rest of that year, any time anything band-related would come up, or the lads asked me did I want to go and rehearse, I would say, 'I can't.' It wasn't that I was avoiding them, it's just that getting my Leaving Cert had become this huge overriding thing that was way more important, which is how it is for most people, I suppose, a big deal. But the pressure I was putting myself under was relentless.

While I was becoming increasingly anxious and more uncomfortable about repeating in the Institute, I did have it in my head that I needed to do well and that that was the whole reason why I was there. So I was just about able to function and keep it together. So while I was stuck in this weird, shy, quiet, majorly anxious mode, I was also fully aware that I had to work hard and get a good result in the exams so I could go to college. This was my fallback plan, that I knew I needed. I spent that whole year trying to concentrate and stay focused while beating myself up constantly, telling myself that I was a failure and trying to ignore all these feelings of increasing discomfort around people.

But I found myself kind of falling deeper and deeper into myself in a way, particularly while I was in the Institute. I was a total loner for the whole of that year, like, I didn't make one single friend. I'd go to the occasional class, I'd take the notes and go sit in a café on my own and just keep my head down. I think I may have talked to two other students in the entire year, and that would have been to ask them what time the next class was. I suppose at the time I just put that unease that I had always felt around people down to nerves. And by trying to avoid them I was just going back to crossing the road, as I did as a kid, whenever something made me uncomfortable. Now that's a real symptom of social anxiety, but to me I didn't know any different. For me, it was just the way I was. I didn't put it down to anything else, like anxiety. But that's what it was. I know that now, but at that point I didn't even know what the word 'anxiety' meant. It had never come into my world.

Now, when I got home from the Institute, back to my parents' house, it kinda went away, particularly when I was on my own. I could go to my room and switch off. I was comfortable in my own company. I'd spend the odd weekend with my girlfriend, and I was okay around her. As far as she was aware, there was nothing wrong. It was like I was living this double life. I was in the Institute and going through this really tough time, but then, when I was with her, I'd be kinda okay. I'd be a bit reserved, a bit shy maybe because that's what

I'm like naturally, but nothing too extreme. And when she asked me how the study was going or whatever, I'd always say everything was grand, even if it wasn't or I wasn't feeling great. I wasn't acknowledging how I was feeling at all.

As the year in the Institute progressed I began to feel even more uncomfortable in class and I was going in less and less. I remember there was the odd time when I had to go and see one of the teachers who would check in with you, to see how you were getting on. And if you didn't clock in at this particular time, or you were late or anything, you got called in. And when that happened I knew it was going to be bad. There were a couple of times when I was a little bit late and I remember, like, having to go in to this teacher to explain myself, knowing that I was going to get in trouble. And with all this other shit that was going on in my head, you know, hanging over me, I'd be there, just shaking. She would say something to me, like, 'Why were you late?' or 'Where were you yesterday?', and I wouldn't even be able to talk. I'd just be stuttering, and mumbling, 'I'm really sorry.' I didn't know it then, but looking back on it now, I was in this state of extreme, constant anxiety the whole time I was there. But it wasn't always twenty-four seven. In a particular moment, I would be incredibly anxious but then, when I got home, and was safe in my room, I was relatively fine. And I had no real insight into what was going on. I didn't understand there was anything wrong with me. I just accepted that that was the way I was. It was only later, after the panic attack, that I'd eventually realise that I might need professional help. If you had asked me back then about having an anxious moment in school, I would just put it down to a specific encounter and not realise there was anything more to it than that.

But every day I went to the Institute those horrible feelings of turmoil and worry and constant fretting were getting ever more intense. I was thinking that even if I got into college I was going to be behind everyone else. Neale was already in college, and so was Bren. I was thinking, *By the time I get there, I'm going to be two years older than everyone else too.* I started to regret doing transition year. *I should have just gone to college, why didn't I work harder last year, even during* You're a Star? Like, I was just putting all this stupid, negative pressure on myself. It's so pointless and when I look back on it now, I wish I could go back and shake myself out of it. But it was too late and I was becoming more and more panicky.

I'm starting to realise, now that I'm thinking and writing about all of this, how much stuff is only now coming back to me. This is the first time I've ever really thought about how I felt that whole year I was in the Institute, so all this stuff, I suppose, that I had buried at the time and had completely pushed aside, I think I'm still processing. And it's tough. It's forcing me to look back on it and I'm experiencing all those familiar feelings again. But I can kinda understand now, feeling the way I did, how it would ultimately lead to this huge panic attack.

I have discussed a lot of things in therapy over the years, mainly just from the panic attack onwards. But to be honest, I have never actually honed in on that time I spent in the Institute and how I felt going in there each day and why I felt the way I did. And what I was actually saying to myself was, *I'm a failure, I'm embarrassed.* I had come to the conclusion that people thought I was a failure and I couldn't face being around them.

I think everybody, to a certain extent, has anxious, negative thoughts but when it's constant, then these negative thought patterns can make you feel miserable. I've learned through CBT (cognitive behavioural therapy) how to catch myself and disarm these thought patterns. The most important thing is to be aware of when it is happening. If you're not aware of it, then it is incredibly difficult to talk about it because you're caught up in it and it becomes an almost normal way of thinking. I didn't have that awareness then.

If anybody reading this can relate to any of what I'm describing, I would suggest talking to somebody.

I was so shy and anxious as a kid that I'd cross the road if I saw anyone I knew coming towards me on the same side. Like, I didn't even want to get on the bus to school anymore because it made me so uncomfortable: *What if people recognise me?* There were always people from Swords on the bus because it was the express straight into town. I'd be very conscious of not drawing attention to myself in case anybody recognised me. I think somebody did say something to me one day, like, 'Are you not your man from 21 Demands? What happened to the band, did it not work out?' They might have been just curious and were asking me how I was, but at that time I automatically perceived it to be a sneering put-down that confirmed my sense of failure. I started to be afraid of the possibility of that kind of encounter happening again.

One day after school I got a taxi home because I just couldn't get on the bus. Dad had given me lunch money and I thought I had the fare covered with the 15 euro or whatever I had. But it was actually 25 or 30 euro by the time I got home. So then I had to go in and ask my dad for the extra cash to cover the taxi. He was saying, 'Why did you get a taxi, why didn't you get the bus?' I told him it was because it made me feel really uncomfortable. He was looking at me, a little bit angry that I had to ask him for money, and when I tried to explain why he just looked confused. It's mad, now that I think of it. It wasn't that I was afraid to get on the bus, it was more like this dread of people recognising me, or trying to talk to me. This would be what's called major social anxiety. I was completely unaware of what was going on but I can see now where all this was headed.

Looking back at that time I spent in the Institute, it almost seems inevitable that I was going to have a panic attack. I had this extreme reaction to the whole *You're a Star* thing and the effect it had on me afterwards. From being up so high, to nothing. I think it hit me harder than I realised. Most other people, like the lads in the band, took it for what it was: a bit of craic, a bit of fun – but for me I was trapped in this overly negative frame of mind. I mean, I've learned through therapy over the years to acknowledge how it creeps in. It's taken years but through therapy I'm now, most of the time, better able to catch myself when I get caught up in this way of thinking. And if I feel anxiety raise its head, I'll become very conscious of upping my self-care, like getting more exercise and maintaining a healthy diet. And making sure I still go to therapy sessions. But still, even now, with Kodaline, like if we play a gig and there's a song that went well but one of us played a bum note, I will completely beat myself up over it. I'd be like, *Shit, what a terrible gig*, whereas in reality we had just played in a new city, in a different part of the world, in front of possibly thousands of people. The whole show had been amazing, the crowd sang every single word, you know, that's the bigger picture, but I'd be focused on this one little thing that went wrong and ignoring absolutely everything else. And for whatever reason, after *You're a Star* I went straight to that: *My music career is over, I'm a failure*, rather than *That was an incredible experience, we're still really young, we can keep doing gigs, who knows what might come of this*. And in the meantime I was going to the Institute, which is, like, one of the best schools in the country. I was lucky, I had great friends, a supportive family … but none of that language applied. It was all just me going straight to the negative, which is a massive part of anxiety. And panic attacks can stem from that type of thinking. Not that I was aware of it, but I had fallen into that trap.

Somehow, despite all this going on in my head, I worked hard and studied the notes. Though I didn't do as well as I thought I would in the exams. I didn't get the points I needed for law in Trinity, which was like 580 plus, or something really high like that, but I did get into economics, politics and law in DCU, which I think was 435 or 445 points, which was still good, 'cause it was a law course. It meant that I could still become a lawyer, but that it would probably take another year on top of that, studying somewhere else or doing a post-grad, possibly, depending on how it went.

But as soon as I got into college I knew for certain that I had no interest in doing law, or in becoming a lawyer. There was no hiding anymore and no escaping the horrible realisation that I was doing all of this for all of the wrong reasons. Neale was there, he was a year ahead of me. He was made for college, you know, he was running around the campus and he knew everybody. Anytime I saw him, and I've never told him this, I'd have this like massive sense of relief because then I was like, *Okay, I know somebody.* He was the chair of the surf and sail committee, and I think the only thing I did do, socialising wise, was go on a trip to Bundoran with him. But outside of that, it was the head down again and not interacting with anybody else, completely lost in myself.

It didn't take long before I stopped going to college. I was too uncomfortable on campus, just majorly nervous and anxious, walking around, not knowing anybody and absolutely unable to meet new people. I don't think I had ever felt that level of anxiety before, where I actually wanted to get out of there. I'd be walking around, getting panicky at the thoughts of just being there. The rational part of me would say, *No, you're in college, just go to your class and study, you're gonna be fine.* But the anxiety that was building up was threatening to overwhelm me more than it ever had before and I just kept trying to ignore it, but it was getting too much.

It got to the stage that I was even afraid to walk on campus. I felt like a loner, out of place, like I shouldn't be there. I knew I didn't want to be there, but I wasn't brave enough to say, 'You know what? This isn't for me.'

My time in college was very brief. I was only there a few months. And as those months passed I turned up less and less, and soon I wasn't even going in at all. I was failing and I knew I was failing. And then my Christmas tests came around, and I did terribly in them, which just strengthened the stick I continued to beat myself up with.

I think my parents could see what was going on and they said I was going to have to get a part-time job, which was fair enough. But then I was worrying about getting a job and then I was beating myself up over that as well. It all just kept building up and building up.

And then it was February, and that's when all this turmoil finally started to seriously affect my college life. I had had enough. I decided then, *Okay, I'm going to drop out*, but I couldn't tell my parents because I knew they would go absolutely apeshit. I didn't even know how I was going to deal with it myself or what I was going to do now with my life. I had already pretty much stopped going to classes and then, when the Christmas exams went badly, I kept the results from my parents.

All these feelings were bubbling up now, stronger than ever before, and they were threatening to overwhelm me but I kept suppressing them, suppressing them, suppressing them until I just couldn't keep the lid on anymore. If people are unlucky enough to be susceptible to anxiety and panic attacks, then holding stuff down and trying to ignore it is not a good idea. That's why it's really important to talk about this stuff, but it would take me years to learn that. But bottling stuff up … eventually it's just going to pop, and that's exactly what happened to me.

I was supposed to be in college when I had the panic attack but I hadn't turned up again. And then everything, my whole life, just flipped upside down.

I was in town the day the panic attack hit me. Well, if you had told me it was a panic attack, at that time I wouldn't have had a clue what you were talking about. To me, it just felt like I was dying. I was with my then girlfriend and we were wandering around, looking for somewhere to eat. She was in college too, and we had been out the night before with some of her friends. We had stayed in one of her college friends' apartments, in the city somewhere, and we had both woken up fairly hungover. We walked into the city centre and it was nice, you know, it was just a nice day and we were having a relaxing time, walking around and checking out the city. We went into a restaurant in Temple Bar, do you know, when you walk across the Ha'penny Bridge and go under the arch? Well, if you keep going, straight across the cobbles, it's just there on the corner, where all the tourists go. It was busy, with lots of people, even though it was a midweek morning in February, but we managed to get a seat and we ordered some lunch. The food arrived and I remember putting down my phone to say something to my girlfriend when this thing came over me ... that's what it was like, like this chill went through me. I stopped, and in my mind I heard the words *What the fuck*, but I was already gone. A wave of like, I don't know, fear I guess you'd call it, rushed up and grabbed me. It was there, I could feel it, in my legs and in my stomach, and it was surging through me, up into my chest and into my head. I pushed the chair back and tried to stand up but my legs were shaking so badly I almost fell over. Slowly, with the room starting to spin, I got to my feet and mumbled something about going to the bathroom. I can't remember if my girlfriend even looked up at me because by now I was too far gone. And I don't know if anyone in the restaurant noticed ... all I knew was that I had to get out of there.

Somehow I managed to get upstairs, with my heart now pumping, and into the men's toilets. I stumbled over to a cubicle, went in and locked the door behind me. By now everything was spinning, my hands were shaking, and I couldn't breathe. Out of the confusion there was one insistent thought: *I'm dying.* I stayed there, both hands pressed hard against the sides of the cubicle, freaking out. I was saying to myself, *It's okay, it's okay, stay calm, stay calm, it's okay, it's okay.* I tried to shake it off, maybe I was just hungover. But the overwhelming feeling was one of absolute dread. I was convinced I was dying. It got to the point where I thought, *I need to get to a hospital.* The room was spinning even faster and my vision blurred so that now I could barely see. My legs went and I kinda crumpled down onto the floor. I just lay there, with my heart beating even quicker and my breathing coming in short, raggedy bursts. I tried to suck in as much air as possible, but it just made it worse. *Oh God, what's happening to me? Help me.* I had to get out of there. Very slowly, I managed to grab onto the toilet roll holder and pulled myself up. I started hitting the lock with my fist and the door swung open. I lunged for the sink, grabbed it and slammed the tap on. Frantically I splashed water on my face, just telling myself to hold on, hold on.

Leaving the tap still running, I turned and got to the door.

Grabbing the stair rail, I got one foot in front of the other until I was back at the table. My girlfriend glanced up and I blurted out, 'I think I'm dying.'

She was like, 'What? What the hell is wrong?'

I just turned and got outside as quick as I could. My heart was racing by now and I still couldn't breathe. I could barely walk, and when she came out after me, I told her again, 'I think I'm dying, I need to get to a doctor, right now.'

She was like, 'What are you talking about, you're not dying.' But she must have seen the look on my face because then she was saying to me, 'Okay, look it's okay, it's okay, come over here, sit down, you're not dying.'

But I needed to get away from there. This whole time my head was spinning and I nearly fell a couple of times. I blindly stumbled up the street, looking for the nearest doctor's surgery while she cried out after me, 'Steve, Steve, wait.' I found a door that looked like a surgery and got upstairs but there was another door at the top with a glass window. I was shouting through the glass, 'Help me, help me, I'm dying,' but the receptionist inside just kept staring at me and shaking her head, no.

I got back outside and I stumbled up another street, trying to find a doctor who would help me. My knees were like jelly but somehow I managed to get to another place. I can't remember where it was but this time I got into the waiting room where there were all these other patients, kinda just looking at me, probably wondering what the hell was going on. I was like, 'I'm dying, I'm dying, help me.' This time a doctor opened a door and told me to get out. Now, when I look back on it, yeah, no wonder he told me to get out. Like, usually you queue up to see a doctor and you wait your turn. So I can only imagine what it was like for that doctor and the patients waiting to see him. They were just sitting there, minding their own business, you know, checking their watches and reading the paper and all of a sudden there's this crazy guy shouting, 'I need to see a doctor, I'm freaking out, I'm freaking out, I need to see a doctor, please, please help me.' I was full-on panicking, panicking, panicking and my head was thumping, like boom, boom boom, and then I remember I was back outside, going, 'Is he just going to leave me here, to die here on the street?' I was thinking, *How could he? I could die right here on the spot and he just doesn't care.* That's how convinced I was that I was dying, like, I was 100 per cent certain of it in my own head. I had never experienced anything like this before … it was all these crazy, physical sensations that had to be related to some serious illness I had but didn't know about. Maybe I was having a heart attack because, like, my heart was racing, or maybe it was some sort of fit, I didn't know, I just knew I needed help. I couldn't have known or understood then how stress and things in your own head could cause such strong physical symptoms but I'm speaking now with the benefit of hindsight. At that moment I was confused and frightened. I just didn't want to die, right there, on the street.

I barged into a few other places, knocking on doors, but I couldn't get in. Eventually I got to this one doctor. I stumbled into the waiting room and did the same thing, gasping, holding onto the wall for support and crying for help. Nobody responded. Some of the patients were just staring at me, like, what the hell is this guy doing? Those poor people, thinking of it now. They must have thought some crazy drugged-up drunken guy had burst through the door. I can't even feckin' remember now where this doctor's was, to be brutally honest. It's such a blur. I think he was on O'Connell Street, up a stairs, on the corner? But I could be wrong. This time the receptionist stood up and said, 'Okay, calm down, calm down, hold on,' and she went and got the doctor.

And then this like really nice calm doctor came out and said, 'Okay, you're okay, come on back here,' and he brought me into his office. He shut the door, sat me down and said, 'Here, breathe into this,' and he gave me a small brown paper bag.

I was looking at him, wheezing, 'Am I going to die? Am I dying, am I dying?'

And he was like, 'No, you're having a panic attack.'

And my first thought was, *What the hell is a panic attack?* But I did what he told me and after a few frantic breaths everything slowed. I could feel oxygen return to my lungs and the pressure in my chest lifted, if only slightly. I got my breath back a little bit and then he was like, 'Okay, what happened?'

I told him, 'I don't know ... I just ... like, this thing came out of nowhere. I think ... I think I'm dying. Like, I'm shaking, my head is pounding, my heart is racing, I feel really weak, I feel lightheaded, I can't really stand up, I'm freaking out, I don't know what the hell is going on. Can you just, can you help me, please? Can you check, can you just tell me what's going on?'

And he very gently said, 'I think you're having a panic attack, you'll be okay. It's just stress, it's all in your head.'

And in that moment the tension eased a tiny bit, even though none of it was making any sense ... how could this all be just in my head? I couldn't understand how this could all be in my head if I was physically shaking and having trouble breathing. He explained a bit more about what it was and how the physical symptoms stem from the thoughts in your head. I did calm down a little bit because he's a doctor, right, and he knows what he's talking about, so I mustn't be dying. He examined me a bit further and then he goes, 'Here, take these,' and he gave me some small blue tablets in a packet with the word Xanax on it. He told me they would help, that I'd be okay and that I should come back to him in a day or two.

These were benzos, as I'd learn later, which are sometimes prescribed for easing anxiety. I put them in my pocket and walked out to see my girlfriend there in the waiting room, looking scared. I was still rattled and very confused. She was asking me was I okay and I just nodded, without saying anything. We got outside and we must have got the bus back to Swords, but I can't remember, it's all a bit blurry. From what I recall she was very supportive, she was like, 'Are you okay? I hope you're okay, you'll be alright.' We got back to Swords, and when I reached my house I remember still being absolutely shattered. It was like this panic attack had happened and my anxiety levels were now 10 times what they had been before … and they stayed like that. I wanted to go to my dad and try to explain what had happened. But I wasn't even sure I knew myself what was going on. And I was afraid of showing him the pills the doctor had given me. My dad worked in a psychiatric hospital and had seen the extremes of mental illness. For 30 years he was around people who had incurable psychotic illnesses. And he would have known about certain types of medication and the possible negative effects it could have on people. For all I knew, this Xanax was the same thing, and I thought that if I showed them to him he might think I needed to be hospitalised too. I know it doesn't make much sense now but that was how I was thinking at that moment. So instead I went upstairs and into my room, the attic where I slept, and threw them in the bin. I lay down on the bed. My head was spinning. I was just lying there, staring at the ceiling, crying, and thinking, *My life is over.* I didn't know what was going on but obviously there was something seriously wrong with me. I was thinking, *If all this is in my head, how the hell am I supposed to fix that?* And that thought just made it worse. I was confused … I felt like I hadn't done anything wrong. I couldn't make sense of what had just happened to me. When I look back on it now I can understand why I had that panic attack. I can see all the stressors that were there, like failing college, beating myself up constantly, blaming myself for the band not working out … but I was completely oblivious to any rational thought.

I never did go back to that doctor; I was too frightened. And I didn't speak to my parents either; in fact, it would take me years to ever open up to anybody. I decided there and then that I was just going to have to suck it up. I was thinking, *Whatever has happened to me, I'm going to have to deal with it, on my own,* which is, like, the completely wrong thing to do.

And now it was like I was stuck in this state, with this constant on-the-edge, about-to-absolutely-lose-it sense of fear. It wasn't like I had this one big panic attack and then afterwards I calmed down a bit. The sense of panic was still way up there, and it didn't go back down. I was left thinking that whatever this is, I'm going to be stuck with it forever. It's never going to go away and I'll never be the same again. I had no idea if I would ever be able to get out of this. It was an absolutely horrible, horrible, frightening feeling.

7

TWO DAYS AFTER THE PANIC ATTACK I WAS still in this state of absolute heightened fear and anxiety. All those extreme sensations that I suffered while having the panic attack – you know, the racing heart, the panicky feeling, the headaches – were all still there. And they weren't easing off; if anything, they were getting worse. I had a severe pain in my chest and it felt like I couldn't breathe properly. There were all these other symptoms too: I was dizzy and lightheaded. I had slightly blurred vison and it felt like my hands were trembling. I didn't know what it all meant but because I had had them since the panic attack and they weren't going away, it convinced me that there was something seriously wrong with me. At least before the panic attack happened, whenever I was feeling all that incredible discomfort, when I got home to my house or I was in my room or with my then girlfriend or someone I knew, I'd feel slightly better. I hid what I was going through from my parents, worried that I'd frighten them. But now, ever since the panic attack, it was just full-on, twenty-four seven. There was no escape from it. I was trapped in this crazy, nervous, shaky mode and it stayed that way. It felt like something had snapped inside me. I had tumbling, racing thoughts, such as *This can't just be all in my head, how can I be experiencing all these physical symptoms if it's all in my head? There must be something physically wrong with me.* I didn't know what was happening to me but I was convinced I was dying.

I couldn't stand it anymore. I think it was like a Friday that I had the panic attack and then on the Sunday I quietly asked my sister Denise to take me to A&E. She was the only sibling who could drive and I didn't want to ask my parents because I didn't want to freak them out. She asked me what was wrong but I couldn't explain it to her.

She brought me to the hospital and I remember the whole time in the waiting area just sitting there, like, quietly freaking out. It wasn't a full-blown panic attack but it was like this persistent, sharp fear was there the whole time. It was like I was on the verge of having a massive breakdown. I was stuck in this major anxious mode and I kept thinking, *Oh my God, if I don't get seen to now, I might die.*

I thought I was going to pass out if somebody didn't come and see me, and then finally a nurse brought me into a room. I remember lying down on that hospital gurney thing. She was taking my blood pressure and testing my vitals, checking my temperature and feeling my pulse and all that stuff. She was asking me loads of questions the whole time: 'Have you taken any drugs?'

I was like, 'No, I don't do drugs.'

'Have you been drinking? Did you fall, have you lost consciousness?'

I told her what had happened in town two days before and that this doctor had said it was a panic attack and had given me the benzos.

She examined me a bit more and asked a few other questions and then she said, 'There's nothing wrong with you, you're fine, but it does sounds like you had a panic attack.'

I was like, 'But I had one two days ago. Before that I was fine. And it hasn't gone away.'

She explained that the panic attack was a symptom of severe anxiety. She said I needed to relax and that I'd have to learn how to deal with all this stress that I was obviously feeling.

My sister kept asking me questions as we drove home in

the car but all I told her was that I was okay and asked her not to say anything to our parents.

We got home, and I went straight to my room, climbed into bed and that's where I would stay, pretty much, for a month, with my head spinning and thinking I was slowly losing my mind. I thought it was broken, basically, and I was really worried that my life would never be the same again. I was just thinking all these really heavy, dark thoughts. I think that now, maybe, if I had taken the Xanax, they may have helped, at least in the short term. This is the type of medication you use to stop those physical sensations of anxiety, like some people find them really useful for public speaking, you know, to calm the nerves but they can be addictive and should only be taken when prescribed and not over a long period of time. With hindsight they might have done me the world of good back then at that moment. But I never took them, I was too afraid to. I thought they were for the kind of people my dad had been caring for in the hospital. I was thinking, *Oh my God, I'm going insane. I'm gonna be locked up in a mental institution for the rest of my life*, and that's why I threw the Xanax away.

I reacted like that because I believe there was a stigma surrounding mental health in Ireland at the time. There was that old Irish attitude of, 'What the feck are you talking about, you're crazy.' Thankfully, that has been challenged in more recent years and there is now greater awareness of mental health. We've come a long way since then but for me I was like, *I'm fucked, I'm broken. I can't tell anybody about this because they'll think I'm mad.* I was afraid of being judged. I felt that if people knew or found out that I was on medication for something that was all in my head they would treat me differently. I just kept thinking that shit for a month. I was beating myself up and not getting any better, if anything I was getting worse. It was bad. I thought my life was over because I had never experienced any of these symptoms before. It's not like it was just one panic attack and it was over. The symptoms never actually went away, they just stayed there, getting worse and worse.

But I was left with the feeling that I was going to have to be grown up about this, that I was going to have to suck it up, and get on with it. So that's what I tried to do; I tried to get through it on my own. And that's where the damage was done. I still had this incredible journey with Kodaline ahead of me, but for years I would struggle to keep it together, until eventually this whole anxiety shit started to seriously affect me, like, almost every day, to the point where I had to turn and face it.

When that panic attack first hit me, it felt like it had come out of nowhere. But through therapy I now understand why it happened. Like, in my mind I was failing at everything and beating myself up over it. We were still rehearsing every now and again, but it looked like the chances of getting a record deal or anything like that were gone. We had got a few gigs off the back of *You're a Star*, but it was kinda like our 15 minutes of fame, and then it faded away. Then I had to go back and repeat my Leaving Cert, to get into college to do a course I didn't really have any interest in. As far as my parents were aware, I was moving on. I had given music a go and now I was studying in college and doing well – when in reality I was failing that too, and not only that, I was also keeping it a secret from them. This whole time all I really wanted was another chance with the band, or just to be able to do something in music, but I kinda thought at the same time that it was now impossible. We'd had our chance and now it was gone. In my head I was like, *Alright, well, the band is not working out, I'm not going to be able to do music anymore*. And that plunged me into this really, really dark place and I hadn't even realised it until it was too late. So yeah, I was just this big ball of feckin' stress and worry. But I was ignoring it and then all of a sudden this panic attack happened. It completely changed my life and turned everything upside down.

When I think about all this stuff now, it's obvious to me that I have buried lots of it, deep down, and it's actually making me anxious just going through it all again, which is not surprising. It's bringing me back to that situation, you know, it's kinda triggering. It's tough, but I remember those weeks up in that room, on my own, staring at the ceiling. I'd stay up late and then sleep until the early afternoon. I'd wake up and not want to get out of bed, feeling lost in a really deep and dark place. I was aware that everything downstairs was going on as normal, but I didn't want to go down and face anyone. I'd wait for a time in the evening when everyone had gone to bed, like ten o'clock or something, and then I'd sneak down and make some tea or get some food and retreat back up to my room. When I did talk to my family, I'd try to put on a brave face, as if everything was okay. There was no way I could go into college, and anytime my parents asked me about it, I'd make up excuses. 'Oh, you know, I was told to work on some modules at home,' that sort of thing. I wanted everybody to think that all was fine with me, even though I knew it wasn't. But at the same time, I don't think anybody particularly noticed a change in my behaviour or anything, which I find bizarre now. Nobody ever said anything to me, so that made me think it wasn't obvious to others what was going on. As far as everybody else was concerned, from the outside looking in, I was still just Steve, even though internally I was in turmoil. But I buried it as best I could and hoped I could figure all of it out on my own.

There was one night, though, that I remember from

around that time, when my older sister was having people over. My parents must have been away because everybody was there drinking and stuff. I didn't want to come downstairs, but I did, to say hello. There was someone there who didn't really know me very well. They had seen me and spoken to me, like, two weeks before I had the panic attack and then this was, like, a month later. And they said something to me, like, 'What's wrong with you? You're very quiet, you don't seem to be yourself,' and I kinda got thrown by it. I just felt this surge of anxiety rise up through me as I sat there squirming. I was looking around, shaking my head, saying, 'No, no, I'm fine, I'm fine, I'm just tired,' and I got out of there as quick as I could and scurried back to my room, thinking, *Oh shit, she noticed. She spotted my anxiety, they must know.*

I did kinda mention it to Bren, months later, about what had happened. He didn't fully understand it but he was incredibly supportive at the same time. I didn't really speak to anyone else about it. My sister who had brought me to the hospital doesn't remember much about that time. I only asked her about it the other day: 'Do you remember you brought me to the A&E?' She had a vague memory of it but couldn't recall if it was me she had brought or Dad. I was like, 'No, Denise, you brought me,' but all she could remember was that there was something wrong with me and that I'd said I didn't feel right and needed to go to the hospital. But because I'd hidden it so well, it hadn't registered with her that it was an ongoing thing. And after that night in the hospital, we never spoke about it again. So when I talked to my brother and sisters and my parents at that time, I'd try to be just as normal as possible. I'd talk about everything and anything other than how I was feeling.

It was a very lonely, very isolating place to be. And it's a self-perpetuating cycle, because the isolation and the loneliness make you even less likely to get help. You feel like you have to deal with this on your own. Like, I was definitely caught up in this vicious cycle but I wasn't able to see that I was stuck. It would take me years to realise that. So I spent most of that month in bed and on my own. I'd occasionally go downstairs, nod and say hello and then I'd sneak back into my feckin' cave as quick as I could and just kind of lie there, googling symptoms and trying to figure out what was wrong with me. I knew nothing about mental health or about anxiety, I had never even heard the word before, so I was desperately searching for answers online, like twenty-four seven, and that made things worse, at least for the first while. I would type in things like 'racing heart', 'panicking', 'blurred vision', 'headaches' … all the symptoms of anxiety. And, as you know yourself, when you start googling anything you almost certainly end up convinced you have cancer, or a brain tumour. I was freaking out, going, *Oh shit, what if I have a brain tumour? Oh my God, maybe I do have a brain tumour.* Like, this is textbook anxiety. I still wasn't convinced that I wasn't dying, even after the doctor and then the nurse had said it was just a panic attack. I couldn't accept that. I was like, *But what if it's a brain tumour? They didn't scan me in the hospital for a brain tumour, do I need to go for a scan? Maybe I should go for a scan, just to make sure.* I got lost on forums on the internet, and while you can find all sorts of scary shit on there that will make you feel even worse, there are also places where other people share what they are going through. And the more I researched, the more I realised that there were a lot of other people who were going through something similar. They were describing their own panic attacks and their feelings and a number of them had the same symptoms as I had. And I could relate to some of it. I was like, *Yeah, that's kind of what I'm going through.* And it registered that, yes, there were a lot of other people out there suffering in silence. At least I knew then that I wasn't the only one. And that made me feel not so alone.

That realisation gave me some relief and a tiny bit of space in my mind. Even though I was caught up in all this craziness and constant worrying about everything, worrying that I was dying, worrying about brain tumours, I could try to reason it all out. I had got a second opinion from the nurse, after I had seen the doctor on the day of the panic attack, and they had both said this was anxiety. I'd think, *Okay, I went to a doctor and he told me that it is anxiety. I went to A&E, and the nurse there told me the exact same thing. They're professionals, they know what they're talking about and I don't know shit. I'm going to believe the doctor because he's a doctor.* I started thinking that okay, maybe I didn't have a tumour. The doctor was probably right, you know; if I was dying, I probably would have died by now. I still had all these physical symptoms, the racing heart and the blurred vison, and it was horrible, but I was still functioning. I was still alive. But at the same time I was starting to feel angry, sad and upset. I was like, *Why me? Why did this have to happen to me?* I was only 20 years of age and it felt like my life, as I knew it, was over … what the feck? I would spend the rest of that month in bed, just lying there and feeling really sorry for myself. I was starting to slowly accept that this was actually all in my head. But then a frightening thought occurred to me. *If this is all in my head, then how the hell am I gonna fix that?*

There came a point, after weeks of this, when I slowly started to realise that nothing was going to change if I didn't try to help myself in some way. I was like, *Okay, I can either lie here and feel sorry for myself, wallow in anxiety and all this shit, and a year will pass and I'll still be here, and I'll probably be worse off – or I can actually try to do something that will help me.*

From all my research on anxiety and going on forums, I started to learn about other people's experiences and how they coped. There was a lot of advice about eating well and getting enough sleep. There was also stuff about not drinking too much and avoiding caffeine and that registered with me. There were also discussions and debates about medication but I was too afraid to go down that route. It had crossed my mind that I might need professional help and that was something else that people made a point of suggesting on those forums. But I didn't have any money to pay for that myself and I didn't want to ask my parents. The main reason why I didn't speak to them about any of this was because I didn't want them to know. I felt that if I went to them and said I needed help, that I wasn't feeling right, I'd be letting them down somehow. That was one of the lies that anxiety was telling me. It made me ashamed of how I felt and I didn't want anybody to know. So I decided that I was going to have to deal with this on my own and that if I was going to get any help at all I was going to have to help myself.

One of the suggestions I came across that appealed to me was exercise. I was reading about how it is meant to be one of the best things you can do when tackling anxiety. And it was running, in particular, which was a big piece of advice that kept cropping up. I think people who have anxiety do that instinctively, they run, because anxiety can generate a lot of unwanted energy and running can burn that off. And it was also something I could do off my own bat. I could just go outside, by myself, and run. So I started thinking about going back outside again. And one of the first times I actually left the house, probably after about a month, was to just go for a run.

I'd put on a pair of old runners and a beanie hat and run, and run, and run. I'd run around ten kilometres, pretty much every night. I'd come home exhausted, but that meant I could sleep. Then I'd spend all day on my own in my bedroom. I'd go downstairs when it was dark and go back out for another run. If you asked me, I'd say that running was the single best thing I did, that helped me to literally get back on my feet after I had that panic attack. I got big into it and I would continue doing it for years, from that point onwards. Exercise is incredible, like, I find it amazing and very calming. It uses up all that excess adrenaline that your body produces when you're in the fight or flight mode. This is built into all of us. It dates back to caveman days when a tiger would appear and your body reacted, to fight or run away. The adrenaline starts pumping through your body. It serves a purpose as a safety mechanism but in this day and age, stress can trigger it, like, your boss could say something to you at work and it will set it off. There is no physical danger but your body feels stress as a danger. Exercise, also, as you know, releases endorphins. Every day, to this day, I will do some form of exercise. And if I get overly anxious in any situation, I'll go for a run. Eventually, one of my good friends from school, Craig, started running with me. Myself and Craig would meet up and we would just run, all the way up to Dublin airport and then back to River Valley, which is about eight or nine kilometres. The running gave me a sense of achievement. And so I ran. And I continued running, every single day, for the next three years.

I also started going to the gym. As far as my parents were concerned, I was still in college. But I was never there; I'd pretend to go, but instead I'd get the bus as far as the ALSAA club in Santry. We had a family membership set up there so it didn't cost me anything. I could go in and use all the equipment for free. Between that and the running, they were the only times I got out of the house. I was taking all these small steps on my own, to recover, not that I fully realised that that was what I was doing. I was just trying to do anything to make myself feel better, and running helped, absolutely.

Now, look, it didn't solve all my problems. I've learned that there are healthy ways to deal with anxiety and there are unhealthy ways to deal with it, like drinking excessively. And exercise is obviously a very, very healthy thing to do, but it would eventually come to a point where I was literally trying to run away from how I felt. I was still caught up in these shockingly crazy, anxious thoughts and, as I'd learn years later, eventually you have to actually turn and face those feelings. But I wasn't there yet.

Another thing I was introduced to around this time, by reading about it online, was meditation. I downloaded an app on my phone, a guided meditation app, and I started trying to get into meditation, which I found incredibly uncomfortable at first. I didn't know anything about it, but I thought I'd give it a go because I had read that it was good for you. Today I meditate most days. If I'm ever over-stressed, I'll work out and then meditate afterwards. I find that it gives me clarity, and it calms me down. I listen to sleep meditations at night that help me switch off. Meditation definitely has its place but I was in such a state of panic back then most of the time that it was impossible to switch off. I mean, for meditation to work,

I think it's like exercise, you know, it has to be consistent and you have to incorporate it into your life. I remember the first time I tried to meditate was not long after the panic attack. My parents had gone out to do the shopping or whatever and I was on the computer downstairs trying to find out what else is good for easing anxiety. I was reading about meditation and so I put on some music I found on YouTube and lay down on the couch, trying to relax. I must have drifted off because my parents suddenly came in from the shopping and I was like, 'Shit', and I turned the music off and ran upstairs because I didn't want them to know I was still freaking out.

As the months passed and the heavy sensations eased, I started to feel a little bit more like I had before the panic attack. Still uneasy, but not feeling those extreme waves of fear and panic. I was still going out running, every single night, and I could slowly feel some energy coming back. Don't get me wrong, it wasn't always easy, going out on those dark, cold nights in the middle of winter, when things were really bleak. But it did take the edge off the anxiety, and that made me feel a little bit better, even if it was just for a short while.

I also started listening to music again. When the panic attack happened I was in such a heavy swirl of turmoil that I couldn't even think about music, never mind play the guitar. Alan had gone to study in Galway, and the Fender with the big dent in it lay forgotten in the corner. And when I did put on music I found myself gravitating back to the kind of songs that were on that CD that my dad had made, back when I was a kid. I remembered all those old classics that I had sung along to while I was in the back of the car. Like, there was that Jackson Browne song called 'These Days' that I listened to, over and over again. Neil Young was on that CD too and I was listening to a lot of him. And what else … oh, 'How Can You Mend a Broken Heart?', a cover by Al Green, so it was a mix of kinda old school, mainly slow, ballady kind of songs. I also started to properly get into Bruce Springsteen. The first Springsteen song I ever heard was one called 'Blood Brothers' and that was on that CD. But then of course there's also 'I'm on Fire', and they're two of his slower songs that I found myself going back to. I must have listened to 'I'm On Fire' so many times that every single note was implanted in my brain. There's a lyric in it that just hit me so hard – Springsteen sings about waking up with the sheets soaking wet and a freight train running through his head. How I interpreted that song described almost exactly what I was going through: the cold sweats, you know, the shaken nervousness, the freaking out, not knowing what to do, the anxiety, that constant racing of thoughts and just worrying, worrying, worrying, about everything and anything … that was the freight train running through my head.

But in terms of really getting into Springsteen, that happened through a mate of mine who lived down the road, who I grew up with. Andy is a bit of a Springsteen fanatic, as are most of his family, so much so that he had Springsteen nights where we'd watch the *Live in New York City* DVD, from 2001, I think. Springsteen had done this huge concert in Madison Square Garden, and we must have watched the recording of that live show dozens of times, all the way through. We'd have a few beers and stay up really late and I became this absolutely massive Springsteen fan. I started going into his back catalogue and listening to all his songs. It also kind of made me think about the power of a song and how to tell a story.

As a teenager the music I was listening to had an influence on the songs I was writing, songs that we would go on to play in the band: lightweight, throwaway pop guitar songs. But when I started listening to music again after the panic attack, I lost all interest in that. I didn't know it at the time, but what I needed was music that would give me some peace of mind. I was searching, without realising it, for songs that meant something, that could reach me and help me make sense of this strange new, scary, unsure world I was living in.

The moment that panic attack happened, it completely changed my life. There was Steve before the panic attack and there was Steve after the panic attack. And I don't think I was ever the same person again. But I was slowly starting to function. I came downstairs more, talked to my parents and even summoned up the courage to go over to my girlfriend's house now and again. I was able, to a certain extent, to hold it together whenever I was with her, or members of my own family. I think I did try and explain to her how I was feeling but she seemed more confused than anything. So I just bottled it and never really spoke about it again. I went and hung out with Mark a little bit and we even played guitar a few times. We didn't really talk about the band. I didn't care about music or anything else after the panic attack. I was just focusing on getting myself better. I had given up on college altogether at this stage. I think I went in once after the panic attack but I couldn't even walk around campus. I left straight away, I just couldn't handle being there at all. And then I was like, *You know what? If I fail college. I don't care. I'll figure something out, my health is way more important.* And it was the same as far as the band and music was concerned. I could see what all this worry and stress had caused. I could understand that it was because I had been putting so much pressure on myself. I felt like I had been through the mill already. And I thought, *I can't go through this again*, so I kinda let go a little bit.

I started to get out more. There were a couple of nights

when I'd go over to Mark's and he'd have a few people around. Or we would head to a friend's house where there would be a bit of a gathering. And then we'd go out afterwards, to a pub on a student night, on a Wednesday, for cheap drinks. The first few times I was almost afraid to have a beer when I was out because I thought it would make me worse. But when I did have a drink I noticed that it actually took the edge off my anxiety and I could mix with other people. It helped me to socialise and that's what I did every other weekend for the rest of that year. Nobody I was hanging out with, not any of my friends, or Mark, noticed any difference in me because I'd have a few beers and I'd be chatting away. Now, that could have been the start of a slippery slope, but then the next day I'd be ten times worse. I'd wake up and not be able to get out of bed. I'd be lying there, crippled with anxiety, with the hangover making everything worse. The only way through it was to drag myself downstairs and push myself to go for a run.

As the months passed, I knew I needed to move on. I needed to take care of myself, figure this out, and try to get back to normal. I figured that I'd just fake it and go out there and try to do things that I would have done if I'd never had the panic attack. And one of those things, I realised, was getting a job. All my friends had jobs and were moving on with their lives. My parents were also on at me to go out and get work. I never told them I had dropped out of college. That was the one thing I just couldn't bring myself to do. I'd say it's hard for anyone to do that, to drop out of college while your parents are funding it, so I just buried my head in the sand. Eventually I summoned up the courage to go for a few interviews. And they were absolute disasters. There's something about job interviews that absolutely scared the shit outta me, and the anxiety made it almost impossible. I know it's natural for people to be nervous in some situations, and a job interview is a good example. But for me the anxiety made the process pretty much unbearable, to the point where I'd just be this big ball of nerves. I'd get prepared and go through everything before the interview – *Okay this is what I'm going to say, this is what I'm going to do* – and I'd go over it in my head. But then I'd worry so much about how I was coming across, that that would be my entire focus, rather than what I was actually hoping to say. As soon as I sat down and the interviewers started asking me questions, the whole thing would come apart. I'd just mumble my way through it and stare at my shoes. I'd be sweating and I'd have shaky hands and all that. Then I'd be thinking, *Oh shit, they can see my hands are shaking.* I'd struggle to get even two or three sentences out. Sometimes I'd just give a one-word answer to a question. It would be over before it even started, and they would be like, 'Okay, next.' I'd actually like to look back at some of those interviews to see just how much of a mess I was. I did quite a few interviews that went like that. And it's no wonder I never heard back from any of them. I wouldn't have hired me, that's for sure. I went for a job in a fast-food restaurant called Captain America's in Blanchardstown, when it first opened, dressed in an oversized suit, and I was pretty much a nervous wreck. I think at that one there was a woman and a man interviewing me and the woman said at one point, 'It's okay, don't be so nervous' and that just made me even more self-conscious. And there was one with B&Q, where I didn't even pass the personality test to be given an interview. The state I was in, I'm not surprised. You're supposed to go in there and sell yourself and I could barely manage to say hello. I did get hired as a cold-caller salesman with Sky TV, which is possibly the worst kinda job for someone like me. That was based on commission so I made absolutely nothing for the two weeks I was there.

Eventually, I got a job in a pub through Neale. I had no experience so I pretended that I had worked at this pub where Neale was the owner. I put him down as a reference. They rang him and after asking him a few questions they got back to me and said, 'You're hired.'

It was just a part-time job, a few nights during the week

and the odd weekend. I found it extremely difficult to be there, smiling at the customers from behind the counter and not really knowing what I was doing. I'd stay away from the other staff and go for my break on my own and keep to myself. Occasionally people would recognise me and ask me questions about *You're a Star*. And I'd pretend I had other stuff going on in my life, like college. That lasted a few months and then I got fired when they realised I hadn't a clue what I was doing, but for a little while I had some money to go out with on the weekends. I also did an interview for IKEA, which was opening in Dublin for the first time, and somehow – I don't know how because I was pretty much mute during the whole interview – I got through the first round. They invited me to go for the next round of interviews so I kinda focused on that. I have to say here that this wasn't like I was okay now and I was going around looking for jobs and getting my life back together. All of this was going on while I was still struggling in anxious feckin' misery. But I knew I had to get out there and do things – *I have to get a job, all my friends have jobs* – and my parents were constantly at me to get work also. And I needed the money. But the whole time I was barely keeping myself from falling apart, every single day.

And then we got this call, out of the blue.

While *You're a Star* was still going on we had given Ronan

Keating our demo with the songs that we performed on the show. We didn't know anybody in the music industry so we thought Ronan could help. His manager at the time, Mark Plunkett, sent it to a record company in England, an indie label called B-Unique. They had expressed some interest but nothing had come out of it and we thought that was that. But now they had got in touch again to say they wanted to send a producer to Dublin to meet us. His name was Steve Harris and I kinda knew who he was. Steve Harris is something of a legend in the music business. He's worked with U2, the Dave Matthews Band, Kaiser Chiefs ... From out of nowhere an opportunity had landed in our laps. We hadn't been together as a band for a long time so myself and Mark called the lads and we went over to Vinny's house to rehearse. Before Harris arrived I was trying to think of some new songs to play for him. But I struggled to come up with anything. We eventually met him in the summer of 2009, at a place that is now The Button Factory in town, where we set up our gear in the basement for what's known in the business as a showcase gig. Now, him coming over to see us was a massive deal. It was really exciting, but maybe I wasn't as excited as I should have been. I was like, 'Okay, if he likes us, he likes us,' but I didn't really care. Steve Harris came in, after flying over from the UK, and he was really friendly, like, 'Hey guys.' He was an absolutely sound guy and he had no airs or graces about him, despite his reputation. I didn't really talk to him. It was good that the guys were there. They were able to break the ice when he came in because I was really quiet, even more so than I'd usually be. But the second we started playing I just felt all my energy evaporate. I tried to focus on what I was doing but it just wasn't happening. I'd start a song, the lads would join in, and half way through I'd just stop. The lads were looking at me, like, *Steve, do something*, but I just couldn't get into it. We'd try another song and I'd get as far as the chorus and I'd lose concentration and stop. I don't know what was going on in my head but I just remember that the music didn't feel right. The lads by now were going, 'What the feck are ya doin'? Keep playing.' Then I stood up and said, 'I have to go.' The lads were looking at me like, *What?* I had the second-round interview for IKEA that afternoon and I told them I had to be there for it. Harris seemed confused and he kinda laughed. And I said, 'No, I have to go. I have a job interview.' And he was like, 'Are you serious?' Then I left.

I remember Harris asking me about that session a few years later and why I left when I did. I explained that I didn't think we were any good. At the time he came over we had a lot of songs but they were like those ones we had written as 21 Demands. We were playing all these pop songs and I think, if I'm honest, part of me already knew this was not going to work because I just didn't believe in the music. My heart wasn't in it and it didn't mean anything to me. And what was the point in doing something if it didn't feel right and you had no belief in it?

In hindsight, that should have been that. Harris could've just said, 'I'm never working with these guys again,' but he must have seen something in us. A few months after that showcase gig the record label suggested that just myself and Mark go over to Harris's house in Yorkshire, just to see what would happen, as they put it.

Before we went over, my girlfriend and I split up. I didn't see it coming. I thought we'd been doing okay together, so I was really, really cut up over it. But then again, I was almost resigned to it. I was like, *When it rains, it feckin' pours*. I think that what I was going through – the anxiety and the panic attack and the constant daily struggle – outweighed my ability to keep us together. Relationships are two-way streets, and we might have been fighting a lot, I can't really remember, but it felt like it came at the worst possible time because I was barely keeping afloat anyway. So when she left me I was like, *Great, thanks, I felt like shit before, and now I really feel like shit*. I was dealing with all this stress, failing college and not having a job, and now my relationship was ending as well. It tore me up, just when I was starting to get back on my feet.

Looking back now, it was never really going to work. She was great and all but it wasn't going anywhere. She was fairly well-rounded and sensible and she had never believed in the music thing at all. She was like, 'When are you going to get a real job?' So we were never compatible, but it was my first serious relationship. We had been together for two and a half years, like, I had gone on holiday with her family and all. But the main thing that really got to me after the break-up was that I turned on myself. I blamed the anxiety and blamed myself, 100 per cent, for us falling apart.

I was trying to accept that it was over, that there was nothing I could do about it and that I would have to try and move on and hopefully find someone else. But I was beating myself up over it, and thinking I would never find anybody ever again because I was clearly broken. At the time it was like my world had ended, and it just added to all the shit that I was already going through.

And then, as I was still reeling from the break-up, we went over to Harris's house, in September 2009. He lives in a beautiful little cottage in Yorkshire with his family and I remember walking in and seeing all these discs covering the walls. There was one for Santana in recognition of 30 million sales of their 1999 album *Supernatural*, or something wild like that. When that record came out it was one of the biggest-selling in the world and he'd had a part to play in that. There were all these other discs for other bands that he had worked with and there I was, with my guitar on my back, thinking, *I'm way out of my depth here.* In my head I was like, *Oh my God, this guy is amazing, but I'm not good enough.* And I also knew, in my heart, that we just didn't have the songs. He tried to put us at our ease. He was a really cool guy and he set us up in a mixing room in this amazing studio he has in his house. He was like, 'Okay, guys, what have you got?' but I was totally overwhelmed. I was really excited about all of this but because I knew it was such a big opportunity I was all over the place. And in the end I bottled it. I was just like, 'Eh, I don't know.' I remember Mark getting really nervous and kinda looking at me, like, *Do something*, but I just shut down. I couldn't sing, I couldn't do anything. Harris was trying to encourage me. He was playing a lot of live music while we were with him, Jeff Buckley in particular, and a song by John Mayer called 'Daughters'. It's a masterpiece of a song. And I remember him saying, 'You could do this if you wanted.' But it wasn't working, and afterwards I was heartbroken. This had been a huge opportunity; to get in the room with an internationally recognised, world-class producer was way bigger than *You're a Star*. I was gutted and beating myself up all over again: *Why couldn't I sing? Why couldn't I just start something, anything?* I stayed with Mark in the same room in a B&B in the village near Harris's house. I was feeling really down. And I remember talking to Mark, telling him about the break-up and saying to him, 'What if I never find anyone else ever again?' He was, like, 'What? That's ridiculous.'

I was despondent when I got back home. At that moment it felt like if we hadn't blown all our chances before, we had well and truly blown it now. I found myself in a really sad place. A few nights later I was over in Neale's house with Mark and we sat in the sitting room drinking beers. His dad had this really cool music system. He put on this record by Ted Hawkins doing a cover of a Creedence Clearwater Revival song called 'Long As I Can See The Light' and for whatever reason that just floored me. I don't know if this is true but I heard afterwards that it was one of the last songs he had recorded before he died. And when you think about that while listening to that song it's really mind-blowing. And I suppose because I was in such an emotional state, it really got to me.

I was also listening to this singer-songwriter called Ray LaMontagne. I remember hearing a story about him, that, like, he went to the woods but he had no money and he couldn't get a job. He had his family there and a kid and they lived in a shack in the middle of the forest. It's such a cliché, it's probably not true, the record label probably made it up to sell more records. But the story goes that he figured he had to do something to provide for his family, so he just started writing all these songs that would become his first album. He had this one song called 'Trouble', which was a huge hit. That song really resonated with me too because it's all about your troubles and your worries when you're going through the shit. And I was going through the shit. I was getting more and more into that kinda music I had started listening to again after the panic attack. There was Jeff Buckley's album *Grace* that had all these kind of slow ballads that made me feel better when I listened to them, and I was getting big into Sam Cooke as well.

I don't think I was listening to this music to try and learn what they were doing. I was tuning into it because I was in such a miserable state. I genuinely felt so shit that I started going deeper into these really meaningful, emotional songs … sad songs, if you like, but I was inspired by them. I was spending more time playing the guitar up in the attic and playing the piano downstairs, and, still hurting after the break-up with my girlfriend, I started writing about that. I remember sitting at the piano, playing some chords and singing over it: 'I still hear the sound of that runaway train /

Roll through my heart as lost lover's refrain / But I know in my heart I can never go back / To the way that we were on that runaway track …'

I was sad and angry, resigned and afraid, but I was singing from the heart. I couldn't have known it at the time but this would be the first verse of the song 'All Comes Down'. It's kind of like a gospel song that was influenced by Etta James, who I was also listening to at the time. I remember on one of the rare occasions when we got together to have a bit of a jam over in Vinny's, I brought that song with me. We all played around it and it kinda worked and it would end up on our first album.

There was another day, as I sat in the attic strumming my guitar, when these words came to me: 'All I want is nothing more / To hear you knocking at my door / 'Cause if I could see your face once more / I could die a happy man, I'm sure / When you said your last goodbye / I died a little bit inside / And I lay in tears in bed all night / Alone without you by my side …' I wasn't really thinking about this as a song, I was just trying to make sense of what I was going through. And it felt good to sing these words out loud. But I kinda parked it and didn't really think about it again for a while. But it never went away. It would take a long time, and I couldn't have known this then, but those few lines would become part of what is, to this day, our biggest song and a hit around the world.

It was a few months after that, when I was alone in the house feeling particularly shit, that I wrote another song. But this one came to me all in one go. It was a particularly bad day. I could feel all the turmoil in my mind, and the ill-at-ease-with-myself sensations running through me stronger than they had been for a while. I was just wishing that this was over, that I could go back to the way I was before the anxiety. I was sick of it. Exhausted, I shuffled into the sitting room and sat there, staring at the piano in the corner. I went over and sat down. There was a slight shake in my hands as I ran my fingers over the numbers I had scratched into the wood as a kid all those years ago. I hit the keys and started singing … 'Broken bottles in the hotel lobby / Seems to me like I'm just scared of never feeling it again / But I know it's crazy to believe in silly things / But it's not that easy / I remember it now, it takes me back to when it all first started / But I've only got myself to blame for it, and I accept that now / It's time to let it go, go out and start again / But it's not that easy …'

The words just poured out of me: '… But I've got high hopes, it takes me back to when we started / High hopes, when you let it go, go out and start again / High hopes, when it all comes to an end / But the world keeps spinning around / And in my dreams, I meet the ghosts / Of all the people who have come and gone / Memories, they seem to show up so quick / But they leave you far too soon / Naïve I was just staring at the barrel of a gun / And I do believe that …'

I felt a rush of sadness and pain and then I just broke down. I sat there crying, the tears pouring down my face. I took a really slow, deep breath and then I let it out. I opened my eyes. It felt like a weight had just been lifted off my shoulders.

8

WRITING THAT SONG, WHICH WOULD TURN
out to be 'High Hopes', would prove to be a massive turning
point for me, on both a personal level and as a songwriter. It
felt like I had opened some sort of valve and let all the pain
and anguish flow into the words and the melody. The music
just came to me. I must have written it in less than five minutes
and when I was finished, it was there, in its entirety. And then I
just sat at that piano, drained but with waves of relief washing
over me. I felt a release, like some of the torment that had been
threatening to tip me over at any moment had lifted. I put my
fingers back down on the keys and I played it again, from start
to finish. Then I played it again. And when I finished, I played

it once more. I knew straight away that there was something there. And I was right. As it turns out, that would be one of the songs that would completely change my life.

One of the first people I played 'High Hopes' to was my dad. I remember he was in the sitting room and I called him into the conservatory where I was at the piano, and said, 'C'mere, I wrote this song and I think it's really good, do you want to hear it?' And I played it for him. Now, playing it for someone else, I could feel just how right it was. It was, on a very basic level, a well-constructed song, but it also had this depth to it that summed up exactly how I was feeling. He listened as I sang and when I finished I looked up and said, 'What do you think?'

He was nodding his head and then he said, 'Yeah, it's great, really great, Stephen. Are you going in to college tomorrow?'

I think I just said, 'Yeah.' I realised that for him it was just a song but for me it was the first one I had written in a long time that made me feel better. The lyrics are kinda metaphorical. There's a line about staring at the barrel of a gun. It's quite bleak and maybe it doesn't leave a lot to the imagination. I don't think I was ever suicidal but 'staring at the barrel of a gun' is my way of describing hitting rock bottom. I was also trying to tell myself to keep going, to try and stay positive.

'... I remember it now, it takes me back to when it all first started ...' I was thinking how I got myself into this mess in the first place. '... But I've only got myself to blame for it, and I accept it now ...' I couldn't stay. I had to move on. I had to find a way out. '... It's time to let it go, go out and start again / But it's not that easy ...' I knew it wasn't going to go away overnight. I knew I was going to struggle and it was going to be tough. '... But I've got high hopes, it takes me back to when we started / High hopes, when you let it go, go out and start again / High hopes, when it all comes to an end / But the world keeps spinning around ...' Because life does carry on, you know, regardless of how you're feeling. And like I said at the start of this book, you only get one chance at life and you should do whatever you can to get help if you're feeling down. What I mean to say is, if anybody out there is feeling low, I wouldn't be afraid or ashamed to seek help. In fact, that just shows how brave you are. It was about having high hopes, a belief that somehow, despite everything appearing to be going against you, something good will come to pass.

All these words and melodies were coming from a very deep place, and they were different from all my previous songs. It took me back to when I'd written that song for Colm Maloney, except I was older now and better able to express myself. I could feel that there was something about them that meant something. There was more depth to them than the easy rhyming and catchy tunes of 21 Demands. I had turned again to music in desperation, during what was one of the most frightening times of my life, and after months of lying in the dark I just threw myself back into it. I was writing lyrics and bits and pieces of songs. Anything that would take my mind off the turmoil I was in. As I said before, it was kinda like the only outlet I had, where I could let go and forget about – even for a few moments – what I was actually going through. After lying in bed all night, not being able to sleep, scoured by anxiety and with the freight train running through my head, it was my way of escaping all that. Any time I picked up my Fender and played a few chords or sat at the piano singing, I was lost and the pain was gone. It was an escape and a relief and I would go back to that, over and over again. And now, whenever I sat down and started writing, it was more directly about how I was feeling and about the shitty place I was in.

There was this other melody, and the words I was singing along to it … 'All I want is nothing more / To hear you knocking at my door / 'Cause if I could see your face once more / I could die a happy man, I'm sure' … were about the break-up. I was in bits over it and I wanted her back, but at the same time I knew it wasn't going to happen. And as hard as it was, I had to face up to that fact and move on, and maybe think about meeting somebody in the future. At the same time I knew I was in no state for a relationship. I needed to get a handle on my own issues with anxiety before I could even consider trying to meet someone else.

Those lyrics and that melody would become the song 'All I Want'. I find it very humbling that people play it at funerals. Like, they'll play it for their father who has passed away, or a grandmother, somebody they've lost who is close to them. I suppose that's the power of music. And once you put a song out into the world, it's open to interpretation and in a way it doesn't belong to you anymore. Myself and the guys wouldn't finish that song for another few years. But when it was finally released it would go on to do incredibly well for us as Kodaline. It's still one of our biggest songs to this day. It just grew legs and kept running. It's still going, and has been streamed over a billion times across all platforms.

As the months passed and these melodies kept coming, I had this urgent need for someone else to hear them. I went over to Mark's house and Conor was there. I played 'High Hopes' for them. Conor said it sounded great but that it was like that song 'Little by Little' by Oasis. I dismissed that straight away because I had so much belief in my song. Mark liked it, he was like, 'Holy shit, this is good.' I spent the next few months doing that. I'd write something and then I'd go over to Mark's house a few days later. I'd be knocking on the door, asking his mam or dad, 'Is Mark there?' and then I'd be running in straight away, without even waiting for an answer. I'd rush up the stairs and I'd be like, 'Check this out.' Mark never asked me where all this was coming from, and I never told him. We never really got into breaking down these songs or analysing them, but we both knew that they were different, were completely unlike anything I had done before. They just felt like really good songs and I tried to continue writing like that, about experiences and what I was going through, basing the songs on stories. And, I suppose, it's something that I still do. I'll try my best to tell a story in its simplest form, like most of Kodaline's songs don't have a lot of words in them. Melodically, they're almost like nursery rhymes.

Because I knew in my heart that 'High Hopes' was a great song, it proved to me that I could write really well. I was thinking, *I'm good at this and I wanna do more*, and I didn't care if it didn't go anywhere in terms of, like, getting released as a record or anything like that. It was just something that was making me feel better about myself while I was still in this really shitty place. So when I decided to get another job, after I got fired from the pub, I thought about getting a gig playing music somewhere, in a bar or anywhere that would have me. I needed the money, but all the other lads had their own jobs so it was going to have to be me on my own. I didn't care, at least I could do something that I was interested in.

I literally went around knocking on doors and asking people, 'Any chance I can sing here? Give us a hundred quid and I'll do four hours.' That's what I did. I got to play the odd set here and there but my main gig ended up being in Wright's, who had given us the space for the band to rehearse in during *You're a Star*. Even after they had told us we couldn't use the space anymore, they were decent about it. They had let me keep the PA system and two speakers that we had been using, which was really sound of them. I borrowed a little mixer from Phil so now I had all I needed to set out on my own. I went back to Wright's and talked to Alan Clancy, the manager at the time, about playing a few songs on my own. He said, 'Yeah, cool, why don't you come down and play a set some evening?' That was exactly what I was looking for. I brought the PA system that they had given me and I had a little keyboard as well as my guitar. I'd set up in the wine bar and play there for two, maybe two and half hours, every Sunday. Sometimes there would be nobody there, but after a couple of months I noticed that there were a few people who were coming back, not many, maybe the same ten people. But I figured that maybe they liked what they heard. Maybe they didn't, but in my fragile state of mind it gave me some comfort to think that they did. And I did have a lot of good songs that I could cover. I had a harmonica with me so I could play some Neil Young, like 'Hey Hey, My My'. I had a brace for the harmonica so I could do some Bob Dylan while strumming the guitar. I brought in a few other songs that I'd learned to play as a kid, like 'Knockin' on Heaven's Door' and 'Brown Eyed Girl'. I'd also fill out the set with some Springsteen. There was 'Johnny B. Goode' of course and 'Get Back' by The Beatles, and between them all I managed to fill the couple of hours. I'd also tease out 'High Hopes' when it was quiet, and a few other bits and pieces I had written myself. I had this old blues song that I'd play, to fill any gaps. People would come up and say, 'Hey, what is that? I know that song. Is it Lead Belly or somebody like that?' I'd be too shy to tell them it was something I had put together myself.

It was good, really good. My dad would drive me down with my gear in the back of the car and he'd come in occasionally to sit and watch me play. A few friends would also drop by and give me some support. I really enjoyed it and it helped get me out of the house. Also, I was back playing music and I was getting paid for it too, not much, like I probably got a hundred quid or sometimes 150, but that was awesome.

I'd play from 7 p.m. to around 11, with a break in between, and it would be pretty quiet at the start of the evening. But then, as the night went on, the place would get rammed. All of a sudden there would be a swarm of people coming in for the nightclub that was on later. The wine bar was in this back room and you could hear the dance music booming next door … *boom, boom, boom* … and everybody would be getting more rowdy. I'd be sitting there playing all these mellow songs on my acoustic, surrounded by candles, and I'd be almost completely drowned out by the noise. You'd get a lot of drunken people in, getting hyped up for their big night out, and they'd be like, 'Ah here, would you play something upbeat, would ya? Cheer up, for feck's sake.' I'd always play 'High Hopes' somewhere in the set and I remember this drunken woman coming up to me, going 'Jaysus, would ya play something that's not so feckin' depressing. Do something we can dance to.' And I'd be like, 'Yeah, okay, I'll try.' *Feck*. What would have started off as a nice, relaxed vibe soon descended into chaos.

It was a bit of craic but playing in front of a drunken pub crowd, especially in Ireland, is one of the hardest things to do. People weren't there to see me, I just happened to be in the corner. And the drunker they got, the harder it was to keep their attention. But it's a good confidence-builder, especially when you're playing your own stuff, because people don't want to listen to songs they don't know. And I would advise anybody thinking about getting into music to go and do that, go and play in a bar, especially in Ireland. If you can deal with a load of drunken Irish people who don't give a feck, and who won't be shy in ripping it out of you, especially after a few bevvies, that'll toughen you up, I tell ya. You're the poor guy sitting in the corner with an acoustic singing 'Hallelujah' by Leonard Cohen and there's someone going to the jacks shouting, 'For feck's sake, what's that? Play 'Sweet Home Alabama', man.' But, yeah, it's character-building, that's for sure. It was a steep learning curve but it helped me hone my musical abilities.

And that would lead to a few other gigs around Swords as well, like in The Old School House and The Slaughtered Lamb, and that's how I got by for most of the next two years, playing the odd gig here and there. I even did one in the community centre in River Valley, which was kinda the local. I'd occasionally go there for a pint with Andy, my mate, the one who had introduced me to Springsteen, at the weekend. We'd play cards with some of the other people from River Valley and it was the kind of place where everybody knew everybody else. Somebody suggested that I play there one night and I did. It was funny, like, they even put a sign up outside, '21 Demands … Tonight!' and even though nobody showed up, it was a bit of craic. I played a few songs while they took the piss out of me a bit and then they paid me.

Now they didn't have to, because it was all a bit of fun, but they did, so fair play to them. I'd play in other places too, and depending on how it went I'd go back or move on. If it didn't work out I'd just go back to Wright's because at least that was consistent.

From late 2009 and through 2010, in between playing in Wright's and these other small sets, I'd be at home in the attic or sitting at the piano downstairs, messing around and working on music. Sometimes my parents would get on to me about getting a job, but I'd hold them off by making vague references to going back to college. Other days I'd be over at Mark's, jamming like we had when we were teenagers, for the fun of it. But now I had this mad urge to write more songs that had the same depth of feeling behind them that 'High Hopes' had. And I just needed to keep doing that. I recorded a lot on my 10-track and I'd bring it over to Mark. He was working on a few ideas and riffs too. We spent more and more time working on songs, writing them and recording. We'd record rough demos on the 10-track and any chance we had, we'd get together with Phil, who would work on bringing them up to a more polished, radio-ready standard. We did a good few sessions like that and the songs just flowed. They kept coming, and there was this constant buzz of writing, recording rough demos and doing sessions with Phil and all the while coming up with more ideas. There were a couple of months when, if I sat down for even two minutes, I'd be writing another song. Some of them sprang from the strangest places.

One day my mam arrived home with a mandolin, as a present for my birthday. It's an unusual instrument and I was really curious about it. I was messing around with it and came up with this riff while I was singing over it. I called Mark and when he came over he started strumming along. We figured out some chords and three to five minutes later, we had this new song. We didn't have a name for it so we just called it 'The Mandolin Song'. Around this time I had kinda started seeing this girl but it wasn't going anywhere and I didn't really care. It was kinda like we both knew it wasn't serious so I had written a chorus that goes like '... A love like this won't last forever / But I, I don't really mind, I don't really mind at all ...' So we eventually called it 'Love Like This'.

We got the band together and with Phil we recorded proper versions of 'Love Like This', 'All Comes Down', 'High Hopes' and some other songs. We called up Ronan Keating and he let us use his recording studios out in Malahide, which was a pretty big deal for us as we were broke and could never have afforded studio time. We used it whenever we got the chance, and two of the songs we recorded there over a few sessions,

'High Hopes' and 'Love Like This', would later be released as singles, while 'All Comes Down' also ended up as a track on our first album.

We did a few other sessions with Phil out in Mark's parents' holiday home in Leitrim. It was just the three of us and we recorded and demoed a few new songs. Mark had come to me with this great riff that I helped him turn into a song which became 'Brand New Day'. The lyrics are about making believe that we could leave our hometown, which was Swords, and run away and tour the world with the band. It's about hopes and dreams. It's actually a fairly happy, fun song that has an optimistic streak of hope running through it.

'Well it's your hometown / I think I've outgrown / I wanna travel the world but I, I just can't do it alone / So I'm just waiting on fate to come / … I'll be waiting, waiting on a brand new day…' Funnily enough, that's what we would end up doing, and when we played it in Japan for the first time, at Summer Sonic in August 2013, and sang the tongue-in-cheek lyric 'We could be big in Japan', we all looked at each other on stage and burst out laughing.

We also recorded a song called 'Pray' which is about my grandad, who had passed away a few years before. He was on my mind when I wrote it and in the song I'm asking a question: is he thinking of me wherever he is? Because I was thinking about him. And I still do, to this day: '… I'll pray for you / Do you pray for me? …' It's darker than most of our other songs and it has this very deep feeling to it. It's very special to me.

Mark also had this rough idea that we worked on and fleshed out with Steve Harris over in his place that eventually became the song 'Perfect World', which is now the theme tune to the TV show *Gogglebox*.

We would be recording all these songs with Phil and sending them over to Steve Harris. Even though our previous sessions with him hadn't worked out, that door had never closed. There would be a steady stream of anything we had recorded, songs and ideas, going to him. He'd come back, offering advice and feedback. He was always very positive about what we were doing and that encouraged us to keep going. At one stage he said, 'Guys, I'm a fan.'

I think that must have generated some fresh interest from the record company that Mark Plunkett – Ronan Keating's manager – had also been actively talking to on our behalf. They had heard some of the songs that we had sent over to Harris and they got in contact to see if we would sit down with a writer they had hired, to see if we could work on something together. I was like, 'Holy shit, they're sending someone over to us,' and I wondered if this could be the start of something.

In February 2011, the writer, a guy called James, came over

from the UK for a couple of days. We set up as a full band in Beechpark Studios in Rathcoole, County Dublin. For the first day we all jammed live together, myself, Mark, Conor and Vinny. We played 'All Comes Down' and a few other songs that myself and Mark had recorded, but nothing really stuck. And then on the second day we went to Mark's house where myself and Mark ran through a few more ideas with him. As James was leaving, I told him there was something else I had and I started singing … 'All I want is nothing more / To hear you knocking at my door / 'Cause if I could see your face once more / I could die a happy man, I'm sure …' It was just the verse but he was like, 'That's actually really good.' And then between the three of us we started playing around with it. One of them was singing this melodic part while the other strummed a few chords and then I went … 'But if you loved me / Why'd you leave me / Take my body …' We still didn't manage to finish it, we just added a bit more to it and then left it as it was. But there was definitely something there. James must have gone back to the record label with some good feedback because a few weeks later they invited myself and Mark over to Brighton to meet with him again. I was starting to think that maybe, just maybe, something was happening here. I remember going to my parents just after the writer came over and saying to them that this could happen, that maybe I had another shot at making it in music. By this time I had come clean with them about the fact I had dropped out of college, which they weren't too happy about. They wanted me to go back and focus on my education, but I was saying, 'I really want to give this a go.' I think maybe my dad was starting to accept that music was what I really wanted to do with my life. He was bit more like, 'Okay, go for it,' but at the same time I knew full well that while there might be another chance here, it was only a possibility, and a small one at that. My parents knew this too, so we agreed on a compromise and I reserved a place in law and accountancy in Limerick that was to start later that year. But to be honest, I'd realised by now that, really, music was all I had and all I'd ever wanted to do. I don't think I was ever really going to go back to college and I just couldn't see myself in a regular job, in an office, or even in IKEA. There was always a small part of me that had held onto that dream and imagined 'if only …' and now there was some hope. I was really starting to believe that after all this time, we might be getting another shot here. But at the same time, there were days when I'd struggle just to stay afloat, just about keeping my shit together while avoiding falling into a bottomless pit of despair, which was always there lurking in the background. I was forcing myself to stay positive and at the same time trying not to get carried away.

Myself and Mark travelled over to Brighton to meet with James again, in the early summer. We were only there a few days but we kinda fell in love with Brighton, just the vibe of this cool seaside town. There's a really vibrant band scene there and we were like, 'This is amazing.' I remember thinking it would be so cool to live there. We did a few more sessions with James and got on really well with him, although we didn't really write anything new. But we let him hear a few recordings we had done with Phil that included 'Brand New Day' and 'High Hopes'. James was like, 'Shit, this is really good.' One of the guys from B-Unique, Martin Toher, came to one of the last sessions before we were due to go back home. He had already heard the demos of some of these new songs but I think when he heard them again it set something off. He got particularly excited about 'High Hopes' because he sent us back to Harris's place in Yorkshire to re-record it.

We spent a few days with Harris as he worked his magic on it and took the song to a whole new level. I think that's when the label got really excited because they sent Harris over to Dublin a month later to record the whole band live on it. We went to Windmill Lane and tried to work on it in the studio but it didn't feel quite right. We kind of realised then that we needed a new bass player. It was like a really shit deal but we had to go our separate ways. I suppose we didn't really know then if anything was happening after that. The session hadn't worked out and now we no longer had a bass player.

We were wondering where all this was going, when the label turned around and said they wanted to offer us a publishing deal. The difference between a publishing deal and a record deal is that the record deal establishes ownership of and royalties paid on the recordings made by an artist for a record label. A publishing deal is all about the copyright in the songs and making sure that the songwriter gets paid whenever they're played on the radio, for example. It was a solid offer which also meant that we got an advance for the first time. What we did need was a record deal and that would come later.

But that advance, even though it was small, offered us the possibility that music could become our livelihood. At the same time it meant that we would now have to go out there and prove ourselves. And there was never any certainty that it would work out, I'd learned that already. I mean, how could there be? You can't just write one or two great songs and that's it. It's a much bigger picture with a lot more moving parts in it. And even getting a record deal doesn't mean you've made it. Many, many acts get record deals and never go on to do anything. But for me this was the first official recognition that we were doing something right. And that's when myself, Mark and Vinny decided that we were going to dedicate ourselves to this and see what would happen. The lads decided to jack in their jobs, while I quit my gigs singing in the pubs. In the meantime, I went to my parents and showed them the publishing deal. It wasn't actually signed at that stage because it would take a few weeks to get it over the line, and also they didn't really understand what it was. They were like, 'Well, what does this mean and what is the plan?' They were a little bit confused, but supportive at the same time. Neale also came on board as our guitar tech. He had been working for Coca-Cola at the time so we turned to him and said, 'Do you want to come with us? But you'll have to leave your job.' He did, and Neale is still with us to this day.

We were also debating about what we would call this new band. I think at first we called ourselves 'Radar Love'. I didn't know it at the time but there's a song by Golden Earring called 'Radar Love' which was a big hit in the early '70s. I don't know where Radar Love came from but I think if we had been called that straight away people would have thought we were like this heavy rock and blues band because of the association with that song. In the end we settled on Kodaline. I can't remember how we came up with the name. I think we were trying to find a word that didn't have any associations, so yeah, we were now Kodaline. Some people thought it sounded like some sort of drug you take, like codeine, but we just thought it was simple, and it meant nothing, so we settled on that.

With the advance sorted, we set off for Brighton. We wanted to immerse ourselves even more in this cool town that myself and Mark had fallen in love with while working with James. It took us a while to find a place to stay because anybody who was renting was like, 'Oh, you're in a band?' And we wouldn't hear back from them. I think people just assumed that we'd wreck the place. We'd spend two weeks on a short-term let before we'd have to find another. But eventually we settled down and started looking for a new bass guitarist. We rented a room in a rehearsal space and had a few guys come in but none of them worked out. For most of the rest of the time we just hung out, enjoying our freedom. We were kids and we had just signed our first publishing deal so we had a lot to be happy about. On Halloween night the three of us went out and bought loads of fireworks in a shop and let them off on the beach. We were having a great laugh, and later myself and Mark dressed up as zombies and decided to go to a club, but when we got in we looked around and realised we were the only ones there in costume, which was a bit awkward. On Guy Fawkes night a week later we had a few friends over from Swords and we all got together over a few beers. Phil also came over and he showed me this new app he had on his phone called 'Garage Band'. I was fascinated by it. I went into a room and played around with it and a few minutes later I came out with a song called 'Big Bad World'. It was about us, as a band, going out on our own. I was thinking, *Here we are in Brighton and, holy shit, we're actually doing this*. It was exciting but maybe a bit daunting at the same time. There's this line, 'We go out on our own / It's a big bad world outside / Carrying our dreams and all that they mean / Trying to make it all worthwhile.' So it was like, we're here, we're doing this, we're releasing this music and putting ourselves out there and who knows what's ahead of us. It was about chasing our dreams and hoping it all worked out.

The plan was to stay in Brighton for a few months but it got cut way short, to just a few weeks because we then went straight into recording the *Kodaline* EP and working on songs for the album in Vale Studios in Worcestershire, where we would stay for the next three weeks, in November 2011. It's a residential studio in this big old, beautiful Georgian house that has rooms upstairs where artists can stay. It's owned by this couple, Moira and Chris, and they'd cook food for whoever was staying there. So we'd pretty much be living there, sleeping and eating, while we worked on our music. It was really a musician's retreat. We'd get up in the morning and go downstairs for breakfast before heading into the studio, where we'd spend the day re-recording the songs we already had with Harris. Phil had flown over to help with the producing while Mark was playing a lot of the bass parts on the songs as we still hadn't found a new bass player. For me, this was a dream come true. We were in a world-class recording studio, working on our songs and putting together the album that would become *In a Perfect World*. I think it was hard for me to take in that this was really happening but I was at ease for the first time in a long time because I was so totally immersed in what I was doing. After Vale we went back to Harris's where he was mixing the songs, before going home to Dublin for Christmas.

The first few months of the following year, 2012, would be spent polishing off songs, before recording the rest of the album in Vale, where we rocked up in April, and then in Harris's house the following month. But in the meantime we were still without a bass player. When I was dating that girl who I had written 'Love Like This' about we had gone to a pub in town, on the quays. There was a guy there who was singing with his mate and he had this beautiful voice. He was just playing covers but I could tell he was very talented. I was chatting to him after his set and he reminded me that we had played a gig with him years before. I kinda remembered him. He was a great guitar player as well so when I was talking to the other lads about where to find a bass player, he popped into my mind. I was thinking, what about him? The one thing I knew I wanted, and the lads agreed, was a bass player who could sing. And this guy could sing. Vinny and Mark could already do harmonies so we needed someone who could join in on the chorus to all these new songs. We looked him up online and he had this video of himself covering a Coldplay song that he was playing on guitar and it sounded brilliant. I was thinking that if he could play the guitar that well, he could easily pick up the bass. I got in contact with him to see if he was interested and he was like, 'Yeah, great, I'll give it a go.' I arranged to meet him in town one day and then, just as I was getting on the bus to head in, he called me and says, 'Here, do you know what? I actually can't meet you today.' He told me he had something else lined up and I was thinking that was a pity, because he seemed like a perfect fit. That guy turned out to be Gavin James who, of course, has gone on to have his own career. And in fairness to him I think his talent would have been wasted as a bass player. Even though I was disappointed that we couldn't get him to join the band, the very next day we found Jay, through a friend of a friend. Before we got our publishing deal, Mark had been studying lighting design in The Button Factory, where Dee was his teacher. Dee is our lighting tech guy now and he comes on tour with us. At the time he knew Jay and he hooked us up. We went out to Jay's place in Kildare, where he had a little studio set up. I remember saying to him, 'Let's just do this one song and you do harmonies on it.' So we did this Etta James number, 'I'd Rather Go Blind' and Jay sang along. He didn't even play the bass at that session but afterwards we were like, 'Well, he's cool, he can sing, he's got a good voice,' and that's how Jay joined us.

With Jay on board we flew over to London in March to sign a record deal with Sony. Their offices were in the building owned by Richard Branson that has the famous Kensington Roof Gardens on top. This is where Mick Jagger and David Bowie and all would hang out back in the day and there are even flamingoes that live up there. The Sony people were throwing their annual office party the day we were there and we were asked by Colin Barlow of RCA did we want to play a couple of songs as there were a few other acts performing at it. Steve Harris was there too and he did the sound for us while we played 'High Hopes' and 'All Comes Down' acoustically, and then we signed our deal.

Back in Harris's house we recorded a couple of new

songs in his studio, including 'The Answer', which is a kind of a singer-songwriters' song that means a lot to me. It's an acoustic song about my own insecurities and how I actually didn't have any answers. The chorus is, 'I'm not searching for the answer / I'm not looking for the truth / I'm just talking through a speaker / Because that's all that I have ever learned to do'. That's basically me saying, 'I'm not being preachy here, I don't have the answers, I'm just expressing myself through a PA and a microphone.'

I like that song and it's become a bit of a fan favourite. It's funny, but one night recording in Harris's he had to leave early for a family thing. I felt like I could relax for a second because he's such an awesome presence, and in that one session we recorded 'The Answer' and another one, 'Lose Your Mind'. Vinny had this amazing beat and Mark had an awesome riff that turned into this very trippy, psychedelic song that was inspired by others like The Beatles' 'Lucy in the Sky with Diamonds' and Cream's 'I Feel Free'. When Harris came back he was like, 'Why couldn't you have done that on all the other nights?' We would finish up most of the recording the album in Leitrim, of all places, where two guys, the Cronins, have a small studio there called Transmission Rooms Recording Studios. The recording was pretty much done at this point but we did a few extra sessions there and added a couple of tracks at the end of the album. We also brought a few of our friends down to Leitrim to sing backing vocals on 'All Comes Down'. With the album almost done it was kinda like a celebration and it was a lot of fun.

In June our publisher arranged for us to go over to Los Angeles to do a few showcases, like interviews and stuff like that, which was so exciting for me because not only were we given the chance to play America, but I had never been there before. They rented us a house in the Hollywood Hills for a few days. It wasn't super fancy but we would have been happy sleeping in a cupboard. We played this famous 'School Night' gig in the Bardot, a really iconic venue where loads of industry people would go to check out up-and-coming acts, on a Monday night. To this day it's one of those important gigs to get on. We only played for half an hour, but the following night we played another set for an event organised by Sue Crawshaw, who was working with B-Unique at the time. Sue pitches different songs for TV shows and movies and she rented a place in downtown LA in Soho House and arranged for all these producers of TV shows to come along. We played an acoustic set for these 40 or 50 people and I think someone involved in *Grey's Anatomy* came along and that's how 'All I Want' ended up in one of the episodes. Sue also brought Julian Lennon along, who she was friends with. He came up to us afterwards to say well done and that he really liked our music. I was floored but Mark was like, 'Oh, yeah, thanks very much,' and turned around. After Julian walked off I said to Mark, 'Do you know who that is?'

'No, who?'

'That's John Lennon's son.'

I think Mark's face dropped and then he ran after him to introduce himself properly. Julian was cool. He came to see us when we first played New York the following year, in January 2013 in the Mercury Lounge, where he took pictures of us as we were sound-checking.

From Los Angeles we went to New York for a day to meet the Sony people there. It was just a short visit but I remember chatting to one of the guys about Springsteen because we were both big fans, and he gave me some bootleg CDs. And then the four of us ransacked their record collection. They were like, 'Go ahead, go wild,' and we headed off with as many records and CDs as we could carry.

In September 2012 we released the *Kodaline* EP that had four songs on it: 'All I Want', 'Pray', 'Perfect World' and 'Lose Your Mind'. The record label agreed to fund some videos, so we were going to get one made for each of the four songs. Jono, who had played in my brother's band, introduced us to Stevie Russell, a videographer from Dublin. He heard 'All I Want' and said he had an idea for the video. He had this guy who had like this monster face fall in love with this girl, and he played that character. It was great fun making that video. We're all in it, myself and the lads, we're wearing suits in an office and we got a load of our friends to be extras.

It's such a great video and a few people have told me since how they've cried watching it, 'cause it's quite a touching story and the song itself is super emotional. The first time we watched it, it just floored us. I love the message that it sends out, which, for me, is that you don't judge a book by its cover. It's a real underdog story. The man has this deformed face, he's bullied in the office, and the girl screams at the start when she first sees him. Then it implies they're on a date when she says, 'Yes'. It was Stevie Russell's idea and it matched up so well with the song.

Stevie Russell is a super-talented guy and he's gone on to do loads of other videos for us. He's got a great way of telling a story in just a few minutes. He also made the video for 'High Hopes' and that's another really powerful piece of work. For 'Lose Your Mind', we had this really trippy video to go with it. We didn't manage to do a video for 'Pray', but for 'All I Want' Jono filmed a live acoustic video in this old prefab that was part of a primary school that had been pretty much abandoned in Swords. We had been working on our new sound and rehearsing in that prefab.

But I think it was Stevie's video for 'All I Want' that was really the start of Kodaline, because that really put us out there. It has, like, more than 100 million views now and it got a lot of attention. People like Fearne Cotton and Gary Barlow were tweeting about it and Gary Lightbody from Snow Patrol said it was an amazing song. Fearne played it on BBC Radio 1 as her 'record of the week' and later we got a call from the producers of the show asking if we'd like to come over and do an interview with her. I think she did that off her own bat so myself and Mark went over. Someone from our publishers said we should bring her a present, like something memorable as a thank you, because to get played on a show like that, you know, it was a huge deal.

So we got two goldfish that we called 'Koda' and 'Line' and brought them with us into the BBC. I remember hearing someone say, 'How the hell did they get them in here past security?' Because it was a health and safety issue or something, but we got them in anyway. Fearne was delighted, maybe a bit taken aback, but it was funny, a bit quirky. I think one of the people who worked on the show, one of the producers or something, eventually took them home and they later set up a social media page for the fish. We went on and Fearne told us how much she loved the song and said she had seen the video and cried because she found it so emotional. It was just a short interview but I was pretty much mute the whole time. I was just frozen to the spot. It hadn't really occurred to me until then that to be a musician or to be in a band, particularly the front man, you also have to be able to do interviews. That was kinda my first introduction to it so I was like the deer caught in the headlights: *Oh shit … I don't really know what to say, what if I stumble over my words?* It happens still sometimes, and when it does I lean on the guys and they can jump in and kind of take over the conversation. Mark is good at that and so are the others, they're just more chill than I am.

With the album almost done the label sent us to Rockfield, a studio in Wales, in October 2012, to record the song 'One Day'. Rockfield is an iconic location for musicians and we were blown away by the history of the place. This is where 'Bohemian Rhapsody' was recorded, and where 'Yellow' was written and recorded by Coldplay. There's this wall there, called the Wonderwall, and we were told that was where Liam Gallagher recorded the vocal for that song, outside. The Pixies were there at the same time as us, in the next studio. It was surreal. We were walking past one morning and I saw Black Francis sitting there, drinking a cup of tea. We had a few recording sessions in Rockfield over a week, courtesy of the record label, who were obviously impressed enough by these new songs we were working on that they wanted to treat us. We already had most of the songs for the new album down by now but a few of them, like 'One Day', had come to us really late. Like, I remember I was hanging out with my friend Ciaran after a day in Transmission Rooms studios in Leitrim working on other songs. He had come down for the night and he was showing me a riff. I took the guitar and started playing some chords and singing, 'One day it's here and then it's gone / How are you still holding on? / How are you still holding on? / You've felt this way for far too long / Waiting for a change to come / You know you're not the only one ...' and basically sang the whole song 'One Day' there and then.

I would later work on it and turn it into a song about insecurities and social anxiety. The chorus is ... 'Life passes you by / Don't waste your time on your own ...' For me, it's about trying to deal with these feelings but knowing that life carries on and you have to just keep going. That's what I was trying to tell myself in that song. There's another very personal lyric, '... Too shy to say that you need help ...' And that's about me not speaking openly about my anxiety. I was later told by a friend of mine how he was in therapy and when he mentioned that he worked with Kodaline his therapist told him how he used some of our music in his sessions, particularly 'One Day'. That makes me think about the power of music and how it can reach people who are maybe going through the same challenges as I am.

A few months after the release of the *Kodaline* EP we got a call from a promoter asking us did we want to tour with The Cranberries in France. They were on the French leg of their European tour and were doing all these arena shows when we joined them in November of that year. And it was wild. At the time we were still rehearsing in like, literally, this abandoned school in this old prefab that was practically falling down. And here we were in France, playing to 10,000 or 15,000 people every night as warm-up for The Cranberries.

We had a manager who had come on board at this point and we gathered a crew around us – we had a sound man, a front-of-house person and stuff like that.

So we stepped out on a stage in Paris for our first night on the road with The Cranberries. It was scary as hell. It was a real sink or swim moment for us. We only played for half an hour and it was over before it even sank in what we were doing. And then we were off, following The Cranberries around France. It's hilarious when I think about it now. The Cranberries had such a huge production, like there were all these trucks and multiple tour buses, and then there was the seven of us, crammed into this little white van. It brought me back to the days when we were touring around the country as 21 Demands. At the start The Cranberries' crew – all Irish – were a bit cold towards us, they didn't pay us that much attention. But once they realised we were Irish too they were super nice and really cool and they really looked after us. We'd go on, play 'All I Want', 'High Hopes' ... 'Love Like This' was in there and I think 'Pray' and 'All Comes Down'. We'd only play for half an hour each night but there were a good few gigs. And then we'd jump back in the van and head off to the next city. And it was cool, like we got to see The Cranberries play live each night and they were phenomenal. I'd be watching from side stage as they played 'Zombie' and 'Dreams' and all these other great songs. I think 'Zombie' is one of the best songs ever written. It's so simple but it's so brilliant, and to see Dolores O'Riordan up close singing it at the top of her voice was a special moment, no matter how many times I witnessed it. For the whole tour we kept our heads down. We didn't want to get in anybody's way, because we were incredibly grateful for the opportunity they had given us. But I did meet Dolores briefly. She came up to me one day after our sound check and said we sounded great. And that was it. She kinda kept herself to herself and after that I didn't get to talk to her that much apart from saying hello. But that whole tour was a great experience and by the end of it I think we actually came out a better band, and tighter and better musicians.

In December we got onto the BBC Sound of 2013 poll. Now this was a massive deal because hundreds of people in the music industry vote on which artists will be the ones to watch out for the following year. After Fearne supported us we got on the playlist, and that was the first big thing for us as a band. 'All I Want' started getting some radio play and that led to our other songs like 'High Hopes' getting playlisted. For us, well, for myself and Mark in particular, we would have been slightly obsessed with that poll. I don't know if it's still as relevant now as it was then, but if you came first on it then you were considered a sure thing. The year we were on it I think Haim, who are class, won first prize. We were shortlisted and didn't place but we were still up there with the likes of Bastille and The Weeknd, other acts that would go on to do really well. And to have BBC Radio 1 get behind you in the UK is an amazing thing, because that also affects where you get played in Europe. A lot of the stations like in Holland and Germany and France would look to the BBC playlist to see who is being played and they'll take those songs and put them on their list. I don't know if it's the same now, with Spotify and streaming and all that, but back then it was hugely influential and we felt very lucky.

When our debut album *In a Perfect World* was released in June 2013 we obviously had no idea how it would go down.

All the build-up had been positive, and the EPs released before it went on sale had done well, but we could never have imagined that it would be number 1 a week later and stay there. It was also number 3 in the UK and in the top 10 in Holland.

But to be honest we were so busy that we didn't have a chance to celebrate or even take stock of what was happening.

It was a special moment for us and after that we knew our lives would never be the same again. I'm proud of that album, and it also gave us a chance to pay tribute to one of our friends who meant so much to us. Paul Woods, who everyone knew as Woodzi, passed away at just 22 years of age in June 2012. He had a condition called HHT that he never really spoke about. His family run the HHT charity now and we've done a lot with them over the years to support them and we still do, to this day. I'll make sure to put a link to their website at the end of this book.

Woodzi was a very funny guy and massively popular. He would have been a school friend of mine and I was very close to him, but Mark would have been even closer. Like, he hung around all our houses and he would have been down at the 'Mushroom Tree'. He was in the musicals as well, he was just a big part of our group. Now, his favourite song was one by LCD Soundsystem called 'All My Friends'. It's a dance song but we put our own spin on it and myself, Mark and Phil recorded our version in Mark's attic in July 2012. We got all of Woodzi's friends and our friends to sing on the last chorus. We changed the lyric so it's kinda like we're talking to him. Woodzi used to mess around with Mark, just making little tunes and stuff like that, and Mark had his voice recorded doing a count-in. So we put that on our version, where it's Woodzi counting in the song, and we played it at his funeral. We also made a video for it as well. He was one of our biggest fans. Like, Woodzi was in the video for 'All I Want' and he would have been there at every gig we played after we took off, no doubt. He would have loved that.

So we dedicated our first album to Woodzi and we've never forgotten him. There's another song that we have, called 'Blood and Bones', which only came out a few years ago, and it's about Woodzi. There's a lyric in it … 'And I still drive by your old house / Fight back tears and turn the music loud / Your favourite song by LCD Soundsystem is always on repeat …'

To this day I still think about him.

9

23 August 2013: Reading, England

IT'S MY 25TH BIRTHDAY AND I'M ABOUT TO GO on the *NME* stage at the Reading Festival. The stage is set in a huge marquee and it is absolutely rammed. And it's hot. The sweat is pouring down my face before I even get to the mic. There's also that heavy smell of a packed festival tent, you know, crushed grass, beer-soaked bodies, humid air and mud. I walk out and face Vinny as he starts into 'After the Fall'. I shake a tambourine and then turn around. There's an absolutely massive roar from the crowd. I don't know, there must have been more than 10,000 people there in front of me.

I remember afterwards somebody telling us that the tent had to be closed because there were too many trying to get in. We launched into 'Pray' as the next song and everyone went wild. It's not even a big, uplifting song, it's more like one of those songs that you kick back to and take in. But this audience was so hyped that they started clapping along to it, really slowly. And then when it got to the big drum part they let out another huge shout and sang every word back to us. It was wild. The noise in that tent almost drowned out the instruments, to the point where I could hardly hear the other lads. I was watching some old YouTube clips of that show the other day and I have to say, we sound pretty good. There's a rawness there that I can pick up on. I'm not a great musician by any standard but there's a rough and readiness to those songs that sounds pretty cool. I kinda miss those days. We had an energy then – well, I think we still do, we have our moments, but it has changed a lot over the years. We have a bigger crew now, we have engineers, you know, proper production and big lighting rigs. But back then we were just a band rocking out, and the stage set up was fairly basic. The backdrop we had at Reading, it was just something we got made in the printer's. I think it cost us 300 euro and that probably blew our entire budget. It's a picture of the album, and we'd hang that up, throw our instruments on, walk on stage and rock out for an hour. And that's how we played, from the release of *In a Perfect World* and up to the recording of the second album, when our crew started growing because I think people were beginning to say these guys need to up their production. That Reading show was just one of many festivals we did that year and it stands out because the crowd were so amazing. They went absolutely bonkers.

There had been a similar vibe at every festival we played that summer. The day after Reading, we performed at the Leeds Festival, and before that at Pukkelpop in Belgium and Indiependence here in Ireland. People were turning up in their thousands to watch us play and they would be singing along to all the songs, particularly 'High Hopes' and 'All I Want'. I remember playing 'High Hopes' at Glastonbury for the first time, two months before Reading. I was looking out over the crowd as they sang every word back to us. It literally took my breath away. It was a scene of such wild excitement the like of which I had never witnessed before. We would go back to play Glastonbury the following year where we were on the Other Stage but that first time was on the John Peel Stage. Our publisher had brought us in the day before and we set up our tents right beside the John Peel tent. With our wellies on we went off to explore Glastonbury but we only got to see a little bit of it as it was so huge. We were like,

'Holy shit,' because we would never have been able to go to Glastonbury had we not been playing there. Even if we could have afforded a ticket, it always sells out months in advance. I was blown away by the sheer scale of it. It was like this huge city of lights that had settled over the hills and fields of the English countryside. We went to sleep in the tent and when I woke up I rolled out, completely filthy, and swapped my wellies for some clean boots to go and do our set.

And that's when we thought it had all gone wrong. I was a bit nervous going on stage for this one because there is such an air of expectancy at the John Peel tent, which is, as you know, where all the up-and-coming bands with a buzz around them play.

Everything started okay but what we didn't realise was that the PA system wasn't working. So we could hear everything properly but to the thousands of people in front of us it would have been like we were playing through a very small speaker. They started chanting 'Up, up, up', as in turn the volume up, but to us on the stage it sounded like they were shouting 'Off, off, off'. Our tour manager, who was standing at the side of the stage with a panicked look on his face, did the cutthroat signal with his hand. He was saying, 'Lads, it's not working, get off.' We came off thinking the crowd hated us and that our careers were over before they had even begun. It was a weird, scary moment and I could feel that familiar fear running through me. But then the PA system started working again and the crowd who had been chanting for us to come back on went ballistic and sang every word to every song. Now, that was an amazing moment for me, that was an incredible gig and the crowd were great, but afterwards I went back to the dressing room and hid in there because I was this big ball of nerves. It rattled me but I didn't have long to dwell on what had happened because then we were gone, on to the next gig. And that's what it was like for the whole of that year and the next two years.

We had some amazing moments on that tour, like the festivals we were playing and the other gigs just got bigger and bigger, and better and better. Now, don't get me wrong, we still had some shows where I don't think we played great at all but there were so many amazing experiences happening on a daily basis that there was hardly any time to take it all in. I think that, for me, the sudden rise of Kodaline took me by surprise. What's that expression? It takes 20 years to become an overnight success? It was something like that for me and Kodaline. From 2012 to 2016 it was just full on. We went from nought to a hundred in seconds. When it first started to kick off, I was like, 'Let's do everything.' I wanted to play every gig, and grab every opportunity we got. I think that, because of the let down after *You're a Star*, I appreciated this massive chance we now had. So I jumped at it. We played South by Southwest in Austin, Texas in March 2013, another big showcase festival where loads of industry heads go to check out new bands. We were jet-lagged and still played nine gigs in one week. There was another in Scotland where we played the show and afterwards we met some lads who owned a pub around the corner. So we went there and played another set for the fans who had gathered for a few drinks after the gig. And that's what we did, you know, any opportunity we got, we'd be performing, whether it was at the gig or for the fans in bars before and afterwards, if we could. I remember we came home for one or two days from being on tour and myself and Mark got a taxi and went straight into town, to The Workman's Club, there on the quays. We did what was supposed to be a surprise gig with me on the keyboard and Mark on the guitar but there were hundreds there. It was like that almost every day, through that year and into the next. We were doing it for the pure enjoyment of it and the buzz of it all. And it was great, you know, all of our friends and families were as excited as we were and happy to be involved in such an adventure. People we had gone to school with in 'The Bros' would come to the gigs and we'd all hang out afterwards. Right from the very start we had great support from the people who knew us best. One of our earliest gigs was in The Academy in Dublin the year before, in 2012, and a lot of those who were in the audience were people we knew. But it was at The Sugar Club a few months later, that we noticed all these other people there as well, who we didn't know. We were like, 'Wow, they're actually coming to see us,' and when we got to the end of the set and played 'All I Want' the place just erupted. I was looking over at the lads, smiling and raising my hands as if to say, *What is going on?* It was amazing, it really was. Like, we all grew up together, we were friends, we had all gone to school together and all of a sudden this was happening for us.

Even before our debut album *In a Perfect World* was released in June 2013, the *High Hopes* EP, the Kodaline EP and the single 'Love Like This' were all doing really well. They were getting a lot of airplay on BBC Radio 1 and it just snowballed. We went from playing to 80 people at gigs in the UK to thousands across Europe in the space of a year. In October 2012 we had played support to We Are Augustines, an American band, in small venues like The Ballroom in Birmingham. A month later we were on our own headline tour, where we played the Night & Day café in Manchester, and another place in London that was actually the basement of a bar. That was such a weird gig. There was no barrier between the stage and the audience and there was this woman there. She was standing right in front of me the whole time, staring straight at me. It was really creepy, whatever was going on. Everybody else who was there was really young but she must have been in her sixties. I don't know but it was bizarre. It was around this time that people like Gary Barlow and Fearne Cotton and Gary Lightbody from Snow Patrol were tweeting about 'All I Want' and the other songs and that kind of coincided with that tour. And with the BBC behind us in the UK, giving our songs airplay, the momentum built up and the venues kept getting bigger and we kept touring. There were lots of interviews, on radio stations all across Europe and the UK. Pretty much every day would involve arriving in a new city and going into the local radio station, where we'd play an acoustic set during the interview. Then we'd arrive at the venue, where we'd do the sound check. There would be more interviews before the gig and then we'd be back on the bus, heading to the next place. We were also on a lot of TV shows in countries across Europe. We wouldn't have a clue what they were about but they would have had big audiences in those countries.

In March 2013, we did another tour of the UK that was bigger than the last one and had larger crowds. In Glasgow we played King Tut's Wah Wah Hut, which is where Oasis were famously discovered. It's a very small venue but it's quite iconic. Any artist or band that sells out King Tut's is given a bottle of their own-brand whiskey, and with a full house we shared that with the crew. That tour ended in London in April with one of our bigger shows, in the Scala, where loads of our friends from Swords turned up.

We were just getting our breath back after finishing that show when we were off again on our first proper tour of America. We had played a few one-off shows in the US before, but this was a series of gigs across several states. We were playing support to the Airborne Toxic Event, who I just happened to be a huge fan of. There's one song in particular they have, 'Sometime Around Midnight', which was a big hit for them and I loved it. I think the lads did as well and when we met their lead singer, Mikel Jollett, he told me he really liked 'All I Want', so I think there was some mutual appreciation going on. We were playing to 2,000 or 2,500 people in all these different theatres across these states. It wasn't our audience but they were very welcoming and the gigs were amazing. But I think the touring was even better. We couldn't afford a tour bus so we rented this huge RV instead. We each had our own bunks, and our front-of-house, Cammy, who is basically the sound engineer who mixes the live show, and our tour manager at the time, Lewis Thorn, took turns driving it. It was old and battered and the electricity went loads of times. We broke down everywhere, but that just added to the adventure. I'd write a song about each state we were in or each city, as a challenge, because we had a lot of time on the road. It kept us busy because some of those drives across America could be 30 hours long. I came up with songs for Minneapolis, Kansas and St. Louis and Arkansas, and Neale filmed and edited the videos for some of them, that are still online. In Arkansas we stopped off in this RV park in Hot Springs. We had two days off in this middle-of-nowhere place that was owned by a guy called Jimmy Young. He introduced us to a friend of his called Chickenhawk, who was big into music and he managed to get us a gig in this old prohibition bar in town called the Ohio Club, where, he told us, Al Capone used to hang out. The house band that was playing there that night were unbelievable musicians. They were all playing blues music so we decided to do 'Johnny B. Goode'. We were introduced as this band 'Kodaleen ... all the way from Iceland', which made us laugh. They cooked us a big southern breakfast, as they called it, the next day and the local sheriff, Deputy Dan, joined us. They showed us the meaning of true southern hospitality, and it's a memory that still stands out for me because we were strangers who they welcomed with open arms.

We stopped off along the way to visit Sun Studio in

Nashville, where Johnny Cash recorded, and I got really close to Graceland. On the day we arrived at Elvis's old home all the lads got off the RV, but it was lashing rain. It was like this tropical storm had blown in and there was a river running through the car park. I took one step off the RV but my shoes were completely destroyed. I had wrapped tape around them to keep them together because I hadn't had a chance to get new ones, and they started coming apart. Graceland was literally 100 yards away but I couldn't go into the King's house with no shoes on. So I had to get back into the RV while the lads went inside. I never did get a chance to go and still haven't, to this day. I was a bit disappointed but when the lads got back they said it was pretty underwhelming.

I think that was probably one of the best tours we've ever done, because it was such great fun. We'd drive all day and park up by the side of the road or stay in some dodgy motel. There was this one place, I don't even know where it was, but when we got to our rooms the tour manager was saying, 'Stay inside, don't go outside, just go to sleep.' When we woke up we realised we were in a run-down shithole on the side of the road somewhere, and we got the hell out of there as quick as we could. There were a few places like that but for the most part we just stayed in the RV entertaining ourselves and wondering what the next place would be like.

We played in all these cool cities I had never seen before. We busked in Boston and did a couple of shows in New York. I remember after one of them we went to this place around the corner where they offered us a few pints on the house if we played a short set. We made our American TV debut in October 2013, when we played on *The Jay Leno Show*.

But the moment I realised something was seriously happening for us was when we sold out three nights in a row in the Olympia back home, in November of that year. Our debut album *In a Perfect World* had been released in June and a week later it was number 1 in the Irish charts. And now, just a few months later, tickets for some of those shows were going for 800 euro, you know, people wanted them that badly. The Olympia is such a Dublin institution, and in 2020 we were going to do a few nights there, as opposed to doing a big arena show. It was going to be a stripped-down series of acoustic gigs but the pandemic threw everything out the window. I love that venue, the history of it is amazing, and playing a gig there is a particularly intimate experience. But those three shows we did there in November 2013 were surreal. Jay was still quite new to the band but myself, Mark and Vinny would be looking at each other going, 'Do you remember we used to skateboard at the back of Superquinn? How did we get here?' There were many, many moments on stage like that when we'd look out over the crowds as they were singing one of our songs back to us and we'd smile at each other in disbelief.

I think it was around the time of those Olympia gigs that I first met Diana Bunici. We were doing another load of interviews and one of them was on a kids' TV show in Ireland where she was one of the presenters. Diana told me afterwards that she saw us come in. She had heard that we were incredibly difficult to talk to because we would just kind of sit there and say nothing – which, in fairness, was true at the time. Bressie was there as well and she interviewed him instead. And she wasn't wrong. It was a kids' show, all wacky and fun, and we were sitting in the corner with our serious musician faces on as the other presenters tried to get us to engage.

I thought she was really cool and, to be honest, I was very attracted to her. But I was too nervous to go over and say hello. I sent her a message later on Twitter, which is a bit odd, I know, and we kept in contact. Our first actual date was in The Grand Social in town and we chatted for three or four hours about everything and anything and kinda hit it off. She told me afterwards that she wasn't really listening to a lot of what I was saying – and God knows what I was going on about – because she was conscious that one of her false eyelashes was falling off. She told me afterwards that she went into the ladies to check but to her horror there was no mirror there so she couldn't. She spent the whole time with me, worried that her eyelash had fallen off. It took a lot of courage for me to go on that date and it was probably a bit awkward at the start, as most first dates are. I was also really happy that The Grand Social was quiet – we were pretty much the only ones there – because I was worried about somebody coming over and recognising me from Kodaline, so that was on my mind too. But I'm very glad that I went on that date. Diana eventually moved to London for work and even though I was crazy busy, we kept in touch every day. Any opportunity I got, when we took a break from touring, I'd try to go and see her. And we've been together ever since.

16 March 2014

It's the day before St Patrick's Day and we're about to play our first ever headline arena show, in Dublin's O2. It was only the one night and it sold out in a matter of minutes. I remember as a kid sitting in the back of my dad's car as he drove past the Point Depot, as it was called back then, and imagining what it would be like to play there. But it was just a pipe dream, something that would have seemed impossible. So to actually get up on stage and play a show at what is one of our city's biggest venues was outrageous. The day before the gig, myself, Mark and Phil were doing a recording session in Swords, working on some B-sides for one of the EPs that we were going to release. Phil was dropping us home afterwards when he said, 'Ah here, lads, get out of the car, quick.'

Myself and Mark were like, 'Why?'

And he said, 'I wanna take a picture.'

We got out and he had us stand outside the O2 phone shop on Main Street, where he took a picture. I think he posted it online somewhere for a laugh with the caption, 'Can't believe the lads are playing the O2 tomorrow night'. That was an absolutely massive gig and an incredible show. Everybody in the place just screamed, singing every word. I had invited Diana along but I didn't even get to see her because the band had to go somewhere afterwards, so it must have been a bit weird for her. It wasn't your conventional date, that's for sure.

By the time we played the O2 we'd already had a hectic few months from January, when we were on *The Jonathan Ross Show*, where we performed 'High Hopes', and were at the European Border Breakers in Holland, where we won the

Public Choice Award. This was a pretty big deal because it was for new bands that had broken out of their own countries. It meant that, like, we weren't just another Irish band, we were actually making waves across Europe – which we were. I remember one of us dropped the actual award and broke it. I think Vinny still has it somewhere. We headed off on another headline tour of the States and Canada in February and appeared on *American Idol*. We were the special guests, and the judges gave us a standing ovation after we played 'All I Want'. I remember Randy Jackson coming up to us afterwards and saying, 'I love your music, you guys are amazing.' It was very LA.

Right in the middle of that tour we were told that we had been invited to perform on *Dancing on Ice* back in the UK. It was too big an opportunity to turn down so we literally had to fly back for just a day and go on the show. We arrived the night before and I remember walking around the hotel lobby at 3 a.m., wide awake because I was still on American time. There was no point trying to adjust so I just stayed awake. We went on the show that night and performed 'High Hopes', completely jet-lagged. The two contestants had a routine to 'High Hopes' and they were gliding by on the ice with your man holding your one while I was still half asleep, trying to stand up at the piano. But it was an amazing experience and after that 'High Hopes' went right up the charts, so it all helped. And then we flew back and continued the tour.

We spent most of 2014 on the road, while I was busy writing songs for our second album in between shows. I was enjoying the experience of travelling and seeing the world, although the anxiety was always there. I tried my best to ignore it, and during the days we would be so busy, moving around from gig to gig, doing interviews and sound checks, that it was easy for me to do that. When I say I was busy, I wasn't even making the decisions. The whole day would be mapped out for me and I'd just go along with it. First thing in the morning, after arriving somewhere, we'd be in a radio station doing an interview, followed by more. Then we'd do our sound check, have dinner – although I hardly ever ate – and then go on stage. I never had a minute to myself. But at night I found it incredibly hard to sleep. That was the only time when I was alone and all the thoughts and worries would come flooding in. I'd have drunk a few beers to try to help me sleep, which is not a great way of dealing with it. I didn't really make any time to exercise or meditate, some of the tools I'd learned to try and cope with the anxiety. I suppose I was masking what was really going on, because of the shame of how I was feeling, and nobody else knew about it. I was always afraid that if I ever spoke out about it, people would treat me differently, so I guess I was still running away from it and instead just carried on. In April we travelled to Australia, New Zealand and Japan. Going there was a surreal experience. There are loads of places I've been to around the world where you can find similarities to somewhere else. Some countries stand out, like Switzerland, which is beautiful, you know, with the rolling hills and the mountains. It's very scenic, but you can still compare it to other places, like the west of Ireland. But Japan, particularly Tokyo and Osaka, the two cities we visited – there is no comparison to anywhere else. They're completely unique. All the signs are in Japanese and it's all flashing lights and very frantic. They have these tiny little bars that you can find down a random alleyway. They're like a little box that can only fit two or three people and sometimes they're stacked three storeys high, one on top of another.

We're not particularly big in Japan, like we've played to 1,500 people in venues that are quite small, but in August 2014 we were on the bill for the second time at Summer Sonic, which is their big music festival. We got the bullet train from Tokyo to Osaka and stepped out to a pretty big crowd who weren't necessarily our audience. But the Japanese really get into their music, they're very enthusiastic and they clap along to every song. But then we noticed that they'd just stop and suddenly there would be silence. Like, you could almost hear a pin drop, to the point where I was whispering over to Mark, 'Can they hear me?'

They are very polite people and they bow down to say hello, but I think it's also a mark of respect. And the lower you bow, the higher the respect, I think that's how it works. I was in a corner shop getting some cigarettes and the shopkeeper bowed down and said 'Hoi!' and then I bowed down and said 'Hoi' back to him. Then he went lower and so did I, until I was slowly walking backwards out of the shop almost doubled over. I love Japan, every time we go there we're well looked after. But you have to be careful of the saké.

In Osaka, there's a bar called Rockrock, it's quite famous and it's where all the bands go after the festival. The first time we were there I got absolutely hammered. I do blame myself but there's also saké. If you've ever had it, you know it's like rocket fuel. Our tour manager at the time and me were like the blind leading the blind, because we were both carrying each other. I slipped down these little stairs and was just lying there when Metallica came out. They were headlining the first year we were playing there, in 2013, and they happened to be in the back somewhere in their own little area. Apparently, or so my tour manager told me the following day because I was too drunk to remember, they came out and had to step over me, as I was lying on the ground. I didn't have many of those crazy drunken moments, you know, I've usually always tried to stop drinking at a certain point but there's something about Japan. Every time I've been there I've had some near blackout moments. I think it's the saké. If you go there, and I'd recommend everyone go there at some point in their lives if they can, just stay away from that rice wine.

In Australia we appeared on *The X Factor*, where our old friend Ronan Keating was one of the judges. He came up to us afterwards and he was saying, 'It's hard to believe you guys were using my shed [as he referred to his studio] in the back of my garden a few years ago. You've come a long way.' 'High Hopes' went into the top 10 and then gold in Australia on the back of that. All the way through 2014 it was one big adventure after another. In June a movie was released called *The Fault in Our Stars* starring Shailene Woodley and Laura Dern. 'All I Want' is one of the big songs in it and I remember when we were back in the States we went to some random cinema in the middle of nowhere. It had been someone's idea to play a surprise set for the audience. We set up our gear and played the song right before the movie came on. But there were only about 10 people there and I don't think they knew who we were. They obviously didn't know our song was used in the movie, you know, so they were like, *We just paid for a movie here, and now there's a band playing? What the hell is going on?*

When we started work on our second album we got an opportunity to record with Jacknife Lee, the famous Irish producer, in his place in Topanga Canyon in LA, which should have been an awesome experience. But that whole session went really badly because I completely just froze up in myself, to the point where I couldn't do anything. Jacknife Lee is an amazing producer, incredibly talented, like, world class, but I don't think he worked with us that well in the studio. He introduced all these new sounds that we had never used before and I think I felt a bit out of my comfort zone. I was really nervous and all those doubts crept in. All the what ifs. *What if I'm not good enough? What if I'm not able for this session? What if I can't sing?* All this negative talk that led to me not even being able to speak when I was in the room with him. It made what should have been an incredible experience into an incredibly bad one. Thinking back now, it didn't have to be that way. It was all just the way I was looking at it. It was really awkward and I think Jacknife Lee pretty much ended that session, which was shit because it seemed to reinforce for me that what I was thinking was correct. But we did end up recording 'The One', which I had written as a present for Phil, for his wedding. When he was getting married I had told him that I didn't know what to get him as a wedding gift, and he said, 'Why don't you write me a song?' I thought, okay, no problem, but then I didn't. The night before his big day he called me and says, 'Is that song done yet?'

I was like, 'Eh, yeah, I'll do it now.'

My mate Ciaran was with me and I sat down and wrote the whole song. I think I just switched off and it came to me. I played it the very next day at Phil's wedding and thought nothing more of it. It was just a song I had written for my friend. But later we were playing a show in Canada and a fan wanted to propose on the stage to his girlfriend. He asked our tour manager and we were like, yeah, of course. So, in the middle of the show, in between two songs, he got her up in front of the whole crowd and went down on one knee and asked her to marry him. She said yes and I said, 'Do you know what? I have this song and it's about true love. I wrote it for my friend, as a wedding present, so I think it will be a good one to do right now.' I played it for them, and two more people in the crowd recorded a video of that performance. They did their own cover of it and put it up on YouTube. When we saw that, we were like, 'This is actually really good, maybe we should record it for the album.' So we recorded it with Jacknife Lee and it became the second single off our second album. Since then, it has become this huge wedding song all over the world. People use it as their first dance, you know, it's just amazing. And it had all started off as just a present for Phil. We also wrote and recorded another song called 'Honest', which turned out to be the first single off that record. I really didn't like it at the time. None of us thought it was the right song to be the first single but the label were like, 'No, it's great, it's upbeat,' so we went with it. But I'm incredibly grateful for 'The One' because I think, if it wasn't for that song, that second album may not have gone on to do as well as it did. It wasn't as big as the first album but it did get a lot of airplay on BBC and it was a step forward, like our gigs got bigger around the world. 'The One' has stood the test of time. I think it has over 100 million streams or something like that now.

But I think the anxiety and the stress that I was feeling at that time is reflected in some of the songs that I was writing. All through this amazing, chaotic time, the issues I had with anxiety had never left me. It was always there, bubbling under the surface. But I was so busy and so caught up in what I was doing, that I could manage, by ignoring it. But I wasn't looking after myself at all. I thought that by just sucking up how I felt and pushing ahead with the band and getting more gigs everything would be fine. But it wasn't and sometimes it caught up with me when I least expected it. There was one night in October 2014 when myself and Diana went to see Ed Sheeran in the 3Arena. It was great getting to watch him live, and afterwards he invited us back to his hotel room. We were just chatting and hanging out there with a few other people and then we left to go for a late drink in that bar Bruxelles, just off Grafton Street. But as soon as I walked in I got hit by a wave of sheer panic that just came out of nowhere. I turned to Diana and said, 'Here, I gotta get out of here, let's just go.' I walked outside and around the corner, to where there's this little lane. I went in there, away from everybody else, and just burst into tears. I had spoken to Diana briefly before about my anxiety but I don't think she had ever seen me like this. I remember telling her that this was an ongoing problem for me. I don't think she fully understood what was going on, but she was very supportive and I calmed down. Diana has seen me at my lowest points, you know, behind closed doors, and she's always been there for me.

But I think in that year, leading up to the recording of the second album, I was putting all this unnecessary stress on myself that I would put down to the anxiety. I was beating myself up, irrationally worrying. I was caught up in my own head, and thinking I wasn't good enough. I put that burden on my own shoulders. I was constantly chasing the next gig, writing the next song, and not looking after myself at all. I know now that you have to take time out for self-care but when you're touring as relentlessly as we were at the time, I was also wondering, *How are we even going to get this album done?* I was thinking we need to get this album done and then go straight back out on the road, which is what we were being told we had to do.

There's one song called 'Better', which is only an album track and not a lot of people know it, but in it I'm talking to the lads in my head … 'Does it make you feel better? / 'Cause it's making me worse / Does it make you feel better? / 'Cause it's making me hurt / Does it make you feel good when I'm falling apart? …' I think a part of me had always hoped that if we made it as a band, if our dreams came true and we made music that people loved, then the anxiety and all the bullshit would go away. It was naïve, yes, but that's kinda what I believed, and when it didn't make me feel better I felt guilty, for not fully appreciating the amazing journey that we had just been on over such a short space of time.

There's another song I wrote called 'Unclear', which paints a really good picture of where I was at … 'When the future's so unsure / When the future's so unclear / We walk, we walk on / Our time, our time will come …' I think it was me trying to tell myself that even though the future was uncertain, everything would be okay. Because I was worrying about failing, worried about this second album not working out. I was overthinking the whole time and self-doubt crept in. I was saying to myself, *What if I can't do this?* or *What if I can't deliver, what if it's not good enough, what if it's not as good as the last record?* To subject yourself to that relentless negative self-talk is incredibly draining.

But I can see with the benefit of hindsight that most of the album was already there. I had been writing a lot on the road, and when we did get into the studio, it was actually done really quickly. And when we needed a third single after 'Honest' and 'The One' I was able to go into another room and write a song called 'Ready' in, like, three minutes. In 'Ready' I was trying to tell myself to snap out of it, to have fun and just enjoy the music. There's a line, 'Never let the pressure overpower the fun'. And this next one is similar, 'Yeah, I'm sure your parents probably said it to you / Follow what you love and you will love what you do / And never let the pressure tell you that you're not / Capable of being everything that you want'.

So it's like, just follow your passion and ignore all the other bullshit. And the title of the song was about me being ready for whatever would come after this album because the first was such a rollercoaster. It was like I was taking a quick breath, and then, *Right, I'm ready to go again*. And when it was released in February 2015, that was the name of the album, *Coming Up for Air*, which pretty much sums up for me what it was like after all the chaos of the previous couple of years.

We spent most of 2015 touring the album across Europe and the US and Canada, from the Festival Big Top in Galway in July, to the House of Blues in San Diego in October. I look back now at our tour schedule and it's full-on. We must have played hundreds of shows that year, as well as doing numerous interviews and TV appearances. In April we went on James Corden's *Late Late Show*. He hadn't really taken off yet at this stage but I remember him coming into the dressing room before we went on to perform 'The One'. The thing that did strike me, as he was chatting away to us, was that he is genuinely a massive music lover, and this is way before he did *Carpool Karaoke*. We had all sorts of amazing experiences that year. In May we did a video with Courteney Cox in her house in Malibu. Our label had introduced us to Johnny McDaid from Snow Patrol, who was engaged to Courteney. We just kinda hit it off and we wrote this song in their house called 'Love Will Set You Free'. Courteney seemed to be a fan of the band and when she heard the song she said she loved it. She offered to shoot a video for it and we even flew over some of our mates to be in it. That was pretty surreal, and as we were fans of *Friends* I was a bit starstruck, but she was cool, you know, really laid back.

Near the end of the year we had two 3Arena shows back in Dublin, in December 2015. These were like two big homecoming gigs for us after almost an entire year on the road and it was a special moment. It was an occasion to celebrate with all our friends and family and we had a backstage party where we had catering for, like, 40 people. It was coming up to Christmas and on the second night we got everybody on stage to sing 'Fairytale of New York'. We invited Imelda May on and I remember her grabbing me and trying to get me to dance. They were really awesome shows and probably, for me, still some of the best gigs that we've ever done, in the way they just flowed, from start to finish, and with everyone singing and dancing. Those shows should have been the highlight of my year – I was at home, surrounded by friends and family and performing for thousands of fans in our hometown. And on the surface I probably appeared to be fine. But I was barely keeping it together. That second night, with Imelda swinging me around and trying to get me to dance, I was laughing and smiling. But what nobody could have known is that only hours earlier I was in a doctor's office desperately looking for help. That morning I was being driven into town with my then manager and my mate Andy, the Springsteen fan, on our way to the gig. Andy lived on the same road as my parents, where I had been staying because I didn't have a house then. I had said to Andy, 'Do you want to come with me and we'll go in together?', and then we stopped to pick up my manager from his hotel along the way. We were chatting away in the car, everyone in good spirits, but when we pulled up in the car park at the back of the 3Arena I just broke down in tears. The other guys were saying, 'What's wrong? Are you okay?' But I just sat there, bawling my eyes out. I was like, 'I don't know what's going on but I really need to get some sort of help.' I was feeling really low. I knew in my heart and soul that these gigs were amazing and I shouldn't be feeling the way I did, but I did, and I needed help. There wasn't a lot the lads could do for me so I left them there while I went straight to a doctor and told him about the anxiety, and how it was nothing new to me. But I also told him that there was this new, unfamiliar low that I was now experiencing and that it scared me. He told me it was quite common for anxiety and depression to go hand in hand. He said if you're dealing with one, unfortunately you can find yourself trying to deal with the other. And I think that's what happened. I had never felt depression before. I was almost fine with the anxiety, I was so used to it. If I had some palpitations or if I was nervous or needed to catch my breath I'd go into a different room and regain my composure. But this was different.

He was very calm and reassuring and he prescribed me some anti-depressants. I left feeling a little bit better and any fears I still had about taking medication went out the window. I just needed something to make me feel better, quickly. I was looking for a quick-fix solution. I thought I would take these tablets and I would be fine. That, of course, is not how it works.

I got through the gig that night but afterwards I just felt burnt out. I had been so busy for so long that I never stopped to reassess and check in with myself to see if I was alright. I just threw myself into it and kept going. I had never learned how to look after myself while I was touring. There was no bracing myself, or taking a breath. There was no real healthy eating or exercise. I had stopped running as well because I couldn't fit it into the endless schedule of gigs, interviews and touring. And that was probably the one thing that had been helping to keep my head above the water. I wasn't really planning my days, it felt like I was just getting pulled along. And there was a lot of drinking going on as well. Like, after every show there would be a full bar there and it's very easy to fall into that. I think I switched to non-alcoholic beers for a while in an attempt to slow it down but I wasn't eating properly either. On tour

I let the lads sort out the rider. I never had any requests or anything, you know, so it was mainly alcohol, crisps and bread and cheese. Sometimes we had catering and then I could have an actual meal but for years I wasn't eating consistently. I never made a point of actually going to dinner or having lunch. So I wasn't looking after myself on a physical level and all the while I was trying to ignore the grip of anxiety that was constantly there.

After that 3Arena show I took those anti-depressants for about six weeks, but I stopped then because, for whatever stupid reason, I was ashamed that I was taking them. I know now that taking medication was a step in the right direction. It was me acknowledging that even in the chaos of all the touring, I needed help. But when I started taking those tablets, for something that was all in my head, it just confirmed to me that something was seriously wrong with me. It made me feel like I was broken. And I didn't want to be broken. It made me think less of myself, when I didn't think a lot of myself anyway. And it made me feel more alienated from everybody else because I was afraid that if anyone found out I was on medication, they would treat me differently.

I remember around this time going to a therapist as well. I talked for a bit and told her about the anxiety and the fact that I had a panic attack when I was younger. She just kind of let me talk and then told me to lie down and picture myself on a cloud as she played some relaxing music. Afterwards I walked out thinking, *This is therapy?* and I didn't bother with it after that. To be honest, though, it was only a half-hearted effort. I wasn't really committing to it. I don't think I was fully ready then to properly try and face my problems. Like with the medication, I was looking for a quick and easy sticking-plaster solution. But I've learned how it's important to find the right therapist, to find what works for you. And since then, I've tried various therapies, like psychotherapy, which I found really tough but beneficial. The sessions got a hell of a lot harder before it got better but it did give me clarity on some issues. I learned about certain things that triggered my anxiety, and why. The one I found very useful and the most helpful, is CBT, which I still do to this day. It's all about catching yourself falling into negative thought patterns and being aware of that happening.

I continued touring and for the most part the gigs were fine. Like, some of them were amazing, and getting to be on stage and singing, doing radio sessions, the promos, all that was great. It was after a show, or beforehand, when all these people would be there backstage, that I'd really start to get uncomfortable. I'd feel trapped and overwhelmed and I was glad the guys were there because they could kind of jump in and talk while I'd step out of the room. I'd try to avoid the afterparties as well, if there were too many people there. Instead I would sneak off onto the bus and just sit there on my own. There were many moments like that when I felt some sort of panic attack was coming on. It never actually got to the point where I had a full-blown attack but I would often have to go away by myself and let the feelings of panic wash over me. I managed, but this was becoming a daily occurrence and sometimes I'd drink a load of beers to try and counteract it and then wake up feeling worse.

But it all came to a head one night in Barcelona, in March 2016. It was a Friday night and we were playing at a place called the Bikini. We had another gig the following night, in Madrid, and then we were off to Portugal. But even before that tour I was excited to go to Spain. We hadn't done that many gigs there up to this point so it was quite new to us. They were some of the first gigs to sell out on that whole European tour so I was curious to see what the fans would be like because there was obviously a buzz there for us.

We arrived the day before and we had that night off so instead of staying on the tour bus we got a hotel. We checked in and I called up my friend Peter who was on that tour with us to see if he wanted to go out and have a walk around. The two of us hung out that night and it was nothing wild, we just went for a few beers. I woke up the following day and from the moment I opened my eyes, it kinda felt like I was on the verge of having a panic attack. Now, this wasn't unusual for me. This was just the old familiar anxiety back again. I was like, *Uh, here we go again, here's anxiety, this horrible feeling. I'll just put up with it, I'll push through and I'll be grand.* Just like every other time. But I just couldn't shake off this really edgy feeling. Over the whole of that day it was there and it got worse and worse. By the time I got to the venue I was feeling really horrible, to the point where I couldn't concentrate. I don't think any of the lads or the crew even noticed, you know, I'd be talking to them and I'd be fairly chill, but in my head I was like, *I need to step out, I need a second, just to catch my breath.* The only way I can describe it is to compare it to an expectant dad who is pacing up and down outside a maternity ward. I was kind of like that all day. I know now that this was my body and my mind saying, *You need to put the brakes on, you need to look after yourself, you need to speak to someone and get help.* It was a warning call but I ignored it.

I put on a brave face, pretending I was fine, and did the sound check. But by now I was screaming on the inside. I lay down, hoping that if I went for a power nap I'd wake up feeling a bit better. But I couldn't rest, and with 15 minutes to stage I was still sitting there, holding onto myself and thinking, *I don't know how I'm going to get through this.* I was trying to talk myself down: *C'mon Steve, you've been through this before, it's nothing new. It's shit, but it's just the way it is. You can do this, you can deal with it.*

Then I started to get incredibly dizzy, to the extent that I had to lie down again. I slumped off the seat and slipped onto the floor. Everyone was there – our tour manager, the lads, all the crew – looking at me while I just lay there. They were like, 'Steve, what's wrong? Are you okay?'

I remember our tour manager, Lewis Thorn, got down on the ground with me. He actually lay down beside me and said, 'You're okay. Can you get up?'

And I said, 'No, I'm not, I'm not okay.'

Now, when I had my first serious panic attack, when I was 20, all those physical symptoms made me believe that I was dying. Because it can feel real, like what I imagine a heart attack would be like. It's a very understandable response for somebody who's never experienced a panic attack before to go straight to 'Oh my God, I'm dying,' and of course that makes it worse. You freak out more, you get dizzy because of the hyperventilation, your breathing goes, it's like you're struggling for air, your heart is beating really fast, your hands are shaky, and your mind is racing. I had many moments after experiencing that first major panic attack when I felt those same strong sensations rise up. But I knew I wasn't dying. I'd be like, *This is anxiety, it's a horrible feeling but it will pass.* I would usually step outside and breathe, or sometimes I would lie on the floor in a toilet cubicle and just wait for it to ease off. And I always got back up again, and managed to get on with it. But for whatever reason this one was as bad as, if not worse than, that first one. The room was spinning so much I was completely disorientated. I could feel my heart pumping, like it was trying to burst out of my chest. Lewis was down there with me the whole time, looking me in the eyes and repeating over and over, 'You're okay. Come on, get up.' In fairness to Lewis, he's firmly of that 'show must go on' type mentality. As he was lying beside me on the floor he reminded me of a gig during the tour in Australia when there was a similar situation and he had convinced me to go on and do the show. He probably shouldn't have because that time I had sunstroke. We had gone to Lone Pine Koala Sanctuary outside Brisbane, where I got to hold koalas and that was amazing. But we had spent the whole day there, under the sun, in boiling hot temperatures, and I'd got a bad case of sunstroke, which can be very dangerous. And my pasty Irish skin didn't help in any way. I was physically screwed. I remember vomiting before the gig and then shitting all over the place as well, so both ends, you know, before collapsing on the ground. Somehow, Lewis had managed to convince me to get up and I sang a shortened set while Lewis and Neale stood side stage with buckets of iced water ready to throw over me in case I fainted. I got through it, I've no idea how, but I did need medical attention afterwards and had to spend like two days in a darkened room drinking lots of water.

But as I lay there on the ground in Barcelona, I knew there was no way I could go on. Lewis was urging me to get up, telling me, 'We've been through this before, we can do it.' I was still lying there, struggling to breathe, with the room spinning. We were supposed to go on stage at 9 and I think it was about 10 past now. Our support band All Tvvins had finished their set, there was a sold-out crowd outside with everybody chanting and cheering, it was loud and noisy, but none of that mattered to me. Finally, Lewis stood up and turned around to the others and said, 'We're going to have to tell them the gig isn't happening.' I think the guys went out, Mark, Vinny and Jay, and I could kind of hear them saying, 'Steve's not feeling well, we're sorry, but unfortunately we're gonna have to cancel the gig.'

I remember hearing the noise of the crowd, letting out a huge groan, there was some whistling and jeering, you know, an unmistakable noise of disappointment. I stayed on the floor as the crowd emptied out. I managed to move over onto a bench and I just lay down on that with a pillow under my head. By now the physical symptoms were so overwhelming that even though a part of me knew it was a panic attack, it got to the point that I told Lewis to call an ambulance. When he told me it was on the way, that put me at ease a little bit. I started to feel slightly better, you know. I still felt shit – anxious, rattled and drained – but my breathing started to come back to normal. My shaking hands and heart palpitations, that all kind of started to ease a bit. The ambulance came fairly quickly and I think by the time it arrived I was already starting to get my breath back. One of our accountants, Sinead, walked me out with her arm around me. I sat down in the ambulance and the two paramedics were asking me what had happened. I was still a bit dazed so they checked me over, and of course they couldn't find anything wrong with me. One of them asked me had I ever had a panic attack and I felt like saying, 'Yeah, every feckin' day.'

I remember feeling so disappointed in myself. I was like, *Oh my God. I could have just gone on and done the gig.* But I also realised that I had a serious problem and it wasn't going away. I had never had to cancel a show before and my anxiety had never got in the way of me performing. I had always found a way to dance around it. I had often told myself that as long as the anxiety didn't interfere with the band or music or performing, I'd manage. Now I knew that road had run out.

Everybody was great, they were all genuinely concerned about me, which I really appreciated. I went on and did the next show the following night in Madrid but for the rest of the tour I stayed very quiet, and kept myself to myself. I'd come along to the venue, do the sound check, and push through the gig. But I didn't drink, and I stayed on my own as much as possible. The whole time I was saying to myself, *Okay, as soon as I get home, I'm going to go to a therapist, I'll go back to the doctor, I'll take whatever medication is required*, because I knew something had to be done for my own sake and sanity. When Diana heard the show had been cancelled and an ambulance was called she came over as soon as she could. We met a few days later in Madrid when the band had a day off and we just spent it together, talking. I was saying to her that I needed to seriously do something about this. I had to fully accept now that I had no other choice but to turn and face my demons head on. When we got back to Ireland we performed what is still, to this day, the biggest gig we've ever played as our own show, at Marley Park in Dublin for 38,000 people.

I remember looking out from the stage that night and there were people as far as the eye could see. There were videos of people after the show, singing on the DART on the way home. It was one of those epic moments in my life when all my fears and doubts vanished for the two and half hours we were on stage. Backstage afterwards, we were all looking at each other shaking our heads, speechless at the magnitude of what had just happened. After a while our tour manager at the time came in, and he had a strange expression on his face. He said, 'Lads, I have some bad news,' and he told us a girl had passed away after she had collapsed at the gig. It was a horrible, horrible moment and we were devastated.

Her name was Ciara Lawlor and she was only 17. We were still in shock in the days afterwards. We went to her funeral and sang at the service. We met her friends and family and then we were talking about what we could do for them. We eventually wrote a song called 'Angel' and Mark put it on a CD and went down and gave it to her parents.

We were saying that if they didn't want it released, then they could keep it, as a gesture, from us to them. But they were like, no, we'd like for her memory to live on, and 'Angel' is now the third track on our third album *Politics of Living* that was released in 2018. We played two shows at St Anne's Park in Dublin the following year and on both nights we performed 'Angel' and her whole family was there. We had a big video screen showing a montage of moments in her life, and that was pretty special. Her family were very touched by that, I think. We all were.

EPILOGUE

I THINK I FELL OUT OF LOVE, IN A WAY, WITH music and touring after Barcelona. For the rest of that year and through 2017 and into 2018 I took my foot off the gas a bit. We did ease off on the touring although we were still really busy, but my focus was more on helping myself. I put myself first and the band second while I actively tried to get better. Music had become a crutch to lean on, even though I wasn't aware of it, but it got to a point where I didn't even want to sit at the piano anymore. I went back on medication after that tour and was on it for about a year. It helped, it levelled me out and took the edge off the extreme sensations of anxiety and depression. I also committed, properly, to therapy. I was spending a lot of time in London where Diana was living and that's where I found another therapist. At the start I had a session once a week and then it was every second week and then it was once a month. I started to feel a little better with the therapy and the medication but I think for the first while I was still looking for a quick fix. I was like, *Why is this taking so long?* And it got worse before it got better. I was confronting a lot of difficult issues in therapy that I'd been simply unaware of. So facing up to all of that and dealing with this baggage that I didn't even know I was carrying was tough. It was months before I got myself back on my feet.

In the months leading up to coming off the medication I got back into fitness, and that has become an important part of my life once more. I started back running, which was just kind of instinctive. It helped and now that, and other exercise, is very important to me because it does ease the anxiety for me. I got big into HIIT workouts and meditation. I watch my diet and lifestyle in general. I'm also very aware of negative self-talk. I'll catch myself doing that now, which makes a massive difference. Now, I can notice if I find myself falling into a slump or a dark place. I can kind of feel it coming on. And the first thing I'll do is book another therapy session, work out, and ease off the pressure by working on songwriting. I'll acknowledge it, rather than try to ignore it. I'll stop and ask myself, *What's going on here? What's causing this?* Now, I still have those moments but I have a better handle on it. Sometimes I'll get up in the morning and look in the mirror and think, *This is gonna be a shit day* or *I'm going to fail at this*, and I have to catch myself saying that. And then I'll tell myself, *It's fine, I'll do what I need to do today and that's all.* I'll offer myself words of encouragement instead of allowing myself to spiral downwards. I still have a lot to learn and I still go to therapy. And that's fine. And if I ever find myself slipping into a deeper depression, or anxiety, I would not hesitate to go back on medication because it did help me.

I have no doubt that I will have more panic attacks in my life. I'm obviously susceptible to them but that doesn't worry me, because I see them for what they are.

In 2017 we chilled a bit, we did a few festivals and worked on our third album. But the pace had slowed and *Politics of Living* was not released until the following year, in September 2018. We probably could've done it quicker, but we didn't, because we weren't rushing into it. And when I got back into writing again I was actually enjoying it. I was writing music for the sake of writing music as opposed to feeling like I had to do it. I suppose, before that, I had been constantly focusing on the next thing: the next song, the next album, the next single. I was always looking to the future, which I still do to a certain extent, but I was better able to sit down and write for the love of it. That album did well, it went to number 1 in Ireland and we toured on the back of it, but it wasn't as relentless as it had been in the years before.

We had established ourselves to a point where we didn't have to do the level of gigging that we did when we first took off. I was excited about getting out there and touring again. But I knew I had to be careful. Barcelona had been a wake-up call. I'd thought I could keep the anxiety under control, but that night proved to me that I couldn't. I realised that if I'd continued the way I was going, God knows what could have happened. I was burning the candle at both ends and I was heading for ... I don't know, but it wasn't good.

I've kinda reset myself, I suppose. I've done a lot to take care of myself since then. Like, every tour I've done since 2017 has revolved around fitness and eating well. You know, simple things that I should have been doing all along, like having breakfast, easing off on the alcohol and getting more into mindfulness and meditation.

It means I put myself first now, not only for my own benefit but also that of everybody around me. Sometimes that means turning down certain things and setting boundaries, which is something that I've had to learn through therapy. Saying no is fine, it's perfectly normal.

Before, we would have had a lot of people backstage, before and after the gig, and I found that very difficult to deal with. When I was on stage everything was fine – as was always the case with me – it was afterwards, when label people and all these other visitors would be there, that I'd be overwhelmed. I'd have to leave the room or I'd just completely fall into myself. I was very conscious that the other guys never had a problem with it, that it was just me. So I would kind of keep myself to myself because I didn't want to step on anybody's toes. I would be worrying about what other people would think if I said anything, so I was putting myself second to everybody else's feelings. It's called people-pleasing. In hindsight I should've been saying, 'Here, look, I need a little bit of personal space,' but I had to learn how to do that. And now what we do is, half an hour after every show nobody's allowed in. You've just come off stage after performing for thousands of people, so you need that breathing space to just chill. That's just self-care, which is important because if you're not looking after yourself you might just end up in a rut and that's no use to anybody, including yourself. And that's not just for dealing with anxiety, that's just common sense.

While we had eased off a bit on the relentless touring and working, we never really stopped. So when the pandemic forced us to come to a halt, it was the first time we actually got to stay at home for any period of time. I live in Dublin now in this house that I bought years ago, but before Covid I could have counted the days I actually spent here.

When Covid first hit, we had to get used to not touring and having an empty calendar. But it's probably been good for us collectively, and for me personally, because I think we needed the break.

It's also given me the time to reflect and an opportunity to sit down and write this book. As I said at the start, it's not something I ever thought I'd do. Because I'm honestly not somebody who wants to be in the spotlight and I never have been. In a weird, messed-up way, it just ended up like that because I love music. I'm obsessed by music. I love it and I live for it but a book is something entirely different. As soon as I started working on it I went back to therapy because I knew that going over some of this stuff would be triggering. So any time I felt overwhelmed I'd bring it into a session with my therapist and talk through it. But I'm glad I did it. I think it has been quite good for me to actually look back and kind of just process it all, perhaps in some ways more than I have ever done before.

I still have issues with anxiety, but I've accepted that now. I know I will have bad times but I think I have a better way of dealing with those moments. And most importantly, I'm no longer ashamed of it. It doesn't define who I am. And I even think that it has helped me, in a very strange way. The one thing I shouldn't have done was ignore the anxiety and try to run away from it. But by doing that it forced me to try and escape. I did that through music and it drove me to keep going. If I didn't have that panic attack when I was 20 I could've gone on to finish college and my life would be very different now. So I'm incredibly grateful for everything that has come my way because of it.

Since Barcelona we've gone on to have these unbelievable moments. I think, as a band, we've gone from strength to strength. Like, the Asian tour we did in 2019 was one of the best we've ever done and the reaction when we went there was completely unexpected. We'd never been there before and we didn't have a clue how we would go down and it ended up being this epic experience. The shows were all sold out, fans were waiting at the airport and we did a press conference as well. It was amazing, taking in Thailand, Indonesia, Malaysia, all these places that I never even thought I'd get to travel around. So to go all the way to the other side of the world and get that sort of reaction was surreal and uplifting at the same time.

And I was there, fully present and taking it all in. I was looking after myself, I was getting up early in the morning, working out, eating breakfast and not drinking. And that's pretty much what I've been doing ever since. For me, any tour that we do now revolves around taking care of myself first and doing a great show. It's about appreciating how lucky I am and how lucky we are as a band, to be able to do what we're doing. Before Covid we headlined a festival in Vietnam and last year we released our fourth album, *One Day at a Time*, which we haven't even toured yet. And even though we're not touring at the moment, we're still working. We had to cancel hundreds of shows, but we're going to go back and do them all. We've more tours to do: European tours, UK tours, American tours, Asian tours. Like, our next Asian tour will be bigger than the last, and it's not a matter of if, it's a matter of when. And it doesn't seem to be stopping. We still have a fan base out there, and there are places that we still haven't got to. Like, we've never been to South America, and there are a few other places I'd like to go to. We're also working on a new record, we have songs to write, and our music is still being used in ads and movies and TV shows around the world. And I feel that as long as the passion is there and there's a will to write and play music, then there's no reason why we shouldn't keep going.

I haven't had a major panic attack since that one in 2016. Obviously it hasn't been plain sailing, there's been tough times and I have had many anxious moments. Usually they come when I'm worrying too much, overthinking and stressing over things. But I've learned a lot about myself. I can kinda tell if I'm slipping into a bit of a low and now I have the tools to counteract it. I'll double down on therapy sessions and just go easy on myself or take a break, which is not something I would have done before.

I don't drink as much as I used to either. I'm wary of alcohol, because if you're in any way susceptible to panic attacks, anxiety or depression, it can make it worse. Now, that's just my story, that's what worked for me, but everyone is different.

And since I started opening up about anxiety and depression I've realised just how many people suffer in the same way I do. It has been truly an eye-opening and touching experience to have friends and so many other people say to me that yeah, they're on medication too or they see a therapist. It's way more common than I would have thought. And I've learned that mental health issues don't discriminate, they affect people in all walks of life, and it doesn't matter who you are or what you do. For anybody who is reading this and who may suffer from anxiety and depression, I hope this might encourage you to realise that you're not alone. I know how it can feel like you're on your own. But you're not. Don't be afraid to get help, even though it might feel like it's the hardest thing to do.

For me, one of the toughest things I ever had to do was admit to myself that I really needed to get professional help. It was very scary but I had no other choice. I'd encourage anyone out there who is feeling the same way to take that step. There is a way out. And there are ways to get better. There are resources and places to go. Don't be ashamed. Don't be afraid.

I'm so grateful for the opportunity that we've been given and that I've been given. To be able to play our songs, write music and perform all around the world, as a career, is incredible.

I don't want it to come across like I did all this incredible stuff but I was feeling horrible the whole time. Even though I've struggled, and still do, I've always tried to appreciate everything that has come our way. Writing and releasing music that people love is a really humbling experience for me. But if I'd never had the band, or written a song, or found my way on stage where I belong, I'd still have had issues with anxiety and depression. I would still have had to turn and face it, go to therapy and get professional help. The biggest thing for me, though, is that I haven't really had any big panic attacks or stuff like that in years, but I have a therapist and if I had to go back on medication I'd do it in a heartbeat.

I've had all these great experiences, travelling and seeing the world, but the journey continues. It doesn't end here. I'm still writing songs and I'm looking forward to working on another album and touring again when all that comes back.

Covid has made us take our first proper break after nearly ten years on the road. In some ways that has been good but at the same time it's got to the point now where I'm like, 'Okay, it's time to play another show.' Because, after all, when it all comes to an end, the world keeps spinning.

ACKNOWLEDGEMENTS

A big thank you to Joanna and Ciara from Hachette Ireland for making this book a reality. It's something I never thought I'd be able to do and without your encouragement and confidence in me, I don't think it would've been possible.

A huge thank you to Neil Fetherstonhaugh for his talent and dedication in getting my story on paper and for putting up with me over the last few months. Again, without you this book wouldn't have been possible.

I'd like to thank my family, friends, and my girlfriend Diana for continually supporting me and believing in me through the tough times. I feel so lucky and grateful to have you, and I know I'd be lost without you all.

To the countless podcasts, self-help books and apps that have helped me and continue to do so. Two podcasts I thought I'd mention are *The Anxiety Coaches* podcast by Gina Ryan and *The Overwhelmed Brain* by Paul Colaianni. Books that I've found really useful are *The Anxious Truth* by Drew Linsalata, *Reasons to Stay Alive* by Matt Haig, *Lost Connections* by Johann Hari and *10% Happier* by Dan Harris. Some apps I recommend include *Insight Timer*, *Woebot* and *Wim Hof Method*.

I'd also like to thank my therapist for helping me to get a better understanding of my issues and for continually helping me to work through them.

I'd like to add a few links to some great charities and organisations that are close to my heart.

- www.walkinmyshoes.ie
- www.cycleagainstsuicide.com
- www.aware.ie
- www.alustforlife.com
- https://hhtireland.org/

To the fans around the world who have supported and listened to Kodaline. You're the only reason I get to write music and do what I love. Myself and the band feel incredibly lucky and grateful to have such amazing support. Thank you.

To Vinny, Jay and Mark – we've had our ups and downs over the years but we've always supported and been there for each other. Thank you for everything.

To anybody out there struggling with mental health issues, I hope you all know that you are not alone and that there's nothing to be ashamed of, so please reach out, seek help and talk.

To finish, I'd like to thank you for reading my book. I hope my journey figuring it all out can help you in some way on yours. Even if it might not feel like it at times, remember: you are never alone and there's great power in speaking up.

Thanks so much
Steve Garrigan